Introduction to Digital Media

Introduction to Digital Media

Alessandro Delfanti and Adam Arvidsson

WILEY Blackwell

Registered Office(s)
John Wiley & Sons, Inc., 111 River Street, Hoboken, NJ 07030, USA

Editorial Office
350 Main Street, Malden, MA 02148–5020, USA

For details of our global editorial offices, customer services, and more information about
Wiley products visit us at www.wiley.com.

Wiley also publishes its books in a variety of electronic formats and by print-on-demand.
Some content that appears in standard print versions of this book may not be available in
other formats.

Library of Congress Catalog Number: 2018029739

Hardback ISBN: 9781119276203
Paperback ISBN: 9781119276210

Cover Design: Wiley
Cover Image: © sudo takeshi / Getty Images

Set in 10/12pt Warnock by SPi Global, Pondicherry, India

Printed in Singapore by C.O.S. Printers Pte Ltd

10 9 8 7 6 5 4 3 2 1

Contents

Preface

Writing an introduction to digital media means opening up a vast field with uncertain boundaries. Digital media have the ability to integrate with all systems of information and knowledge production and to interact with almost every human activity. Their pervasive influence has made them an object of interest for large sectors of the social sciences, economics, psychology, and historical sciences. This book aims to provide a starting point for understanding their social and political significance beyond their role for human communication. To do so, we have done our best to condense into a confined space a vast and complex series of angles and perspectives. Therefore we chose to follow a path that touches upon what we consider to be the core points that it is necessary to cover in order to begin a journey that can lead well beyond the somewhat limited boundaries of this work. The expansion of the digital economy asks for a sustained critical approach to technology, which in turn has led to a significant expansion of research in the field of digital media studies. New degrees, university departments, and journals dedicated to digital cultures and digital technologies are emerging all over the world. The tools they provide to critically interpret the evolution of digital media from a social, political, and economic standpoint have given the social sciences a leading role within this bubbling field. In this book we draw on an emergent and increasingly rich set of empirical and theoretical studies on the role and development of digital media in contemporary information societies. Indeed, the book is informed by international research on digital cultures, political economy of communication, sociology and anthropology of the media, feminist technology studies, and theories on the relationship between technology and society. Furthermore, in many areas we refer to classic social theory and highlight its significance to the study of today's digital media.

Until a few years ago, digital technologies were often presented as good in themselves, harbingers of democracy as well as social and economic development. Digital technologies were said to be bearers of democracy, justice, equality, and economic abundance, allowing individuals to overcome the rigidity of bureaucratic and industrial societies, and providing new possibilities for them to participate in and actively shape the public and productive life. Vincent Mosco described this as the "digital sublime," a myth according to which technologies transcend their social and material reality to become something to blindly believe in. In his words, it was necessary to go beyond this "mythical" vision and thoroughly analyze the cultural, political, and material characteristics of digital media (2004). Recent social and political evolutions have somewhat torn this myth apart. The emergence of ubiquitous surveillance, new forms of worker exploitation, and emerging media monopolies have fostered the rise of a wave of books discussing the "dark sides" of digital media (Morozov 2011). Digital media are often described as a threat to the social order that can potentially undermine the delicate balances that underpin complex societies. With this book we aim at providing some conceptual tools that move beyond these two poles. To be sure, digital media, like every technological innovation that reaches a mass diffusion, have a transformative power. But they can also be used in conservative ways, to preserve existing social and economic arrangements. After all, digital media services are highly privatized, and a handful of giant global conglomerates like Google or Microsoft are in control of most wealth and power. Large corporations like Facebook collect and monetize the information produced by their users, and often collaborate with states and other political agencies to enable pervasive social control. Others, such as Uber or Amazon, create new forms of employment and have the power to influence national and local politics. In order to study the social, economic, and political significance of the digital environment, we need to deal with this complexity. Finally, the diffusion and ubiquity of digital media in our daily lives tend to make them imperceptible, as if we lose sight of their presence and role. In the book we move beyond common sense interpretations of digital media, which tend to portray them in a historical vacuum, according to individual everyday experiences, or the consumer's standpoint, or through ideological lenses.

In fact, the relationship between digital media and social change is a dynamic one. In order to describe its many facets, we describe our contemporary world as an information society: a form of social and economic organization based on practices of information production, manipulation, and distribution. This represents a profound overall change to contemporary societies; to understand it, it is necessary to study the centrality of digital technologies in all spheres of social, political, and economic life. Our choice is reflected in the overall organization of the book. The chapters composing the first part of the book provide the general frameworks for our analysis. In Chapter 1 we lay the ground for an analysis of the techno-social features of digital media. The chapter analyzes the significance of the cycles of evolution of new media, contrasting digital technologies to traditional media such as print or television. In addition, it presents some of the main technological characteristics of digital media and the infrastructures that underpin them. This analysis is supported by an overview of major theories about the relationship between technology and society. In Chapter 2 we introduce the history of information technologies and computer networks, as well as the main theoretical approaches to the emergence of a society based on the production and exchange of information. This chapter is thus developed in the context of forms of globalization of production, organizational practices, and socio-economic arrangements which since the mid-twentieth century have been intertwining with and made possible by technological evolution. The rise of the information society, we argue, is an ongoing process built upon promises and anxieties about the increasingly broad reach of information technologies in all areas of life.

The first two chapters represent the foundations for the following sections of the book. In the second part, we move into the significance of digital media within the social, political, and economic transformations that characterize contemporary information societies. Sociality and the construction of individual identities are transformed by relations mediated by digital technologies. This aspect of contemporary information societies, which we deal with in Chapter 3, is perhaps the most difficult to describe. Each individual belongs to a plurality of relational systems, communities, or publics organized around common interests or passions. Social media are at the heart of this, as they code and structure social relations, allow for a flexible construction of identity, and are the platforms on which new audiences can be organized. In these spaces the boundary between public and private becomes unstable, an important phenomenon for sociality and identity but also for social research and marketing. In Chapter 4 we face the technological and social innovations that allow individuals to use digital media to actively participate in innovation and cultural production. This inclusion has long been a promise of information societies. Widespread digital media and services that facilitate user production have enabled the emergence of new forms of collaboration, from software design, to media content production, to knowledge generation. This is increasingly affecting the production of both services and material goods. Yet the consequences of these phenomena are multifaceted. While digital media have the potential to socialize the ability to produce wealth, corporations are finding new ways of extracting value from social cooperation.

Political power and organizations are affected by these changes through a transformation of the public sphere that we analyze in Chapter 5. The inclusion of new publics means that contemporary politics are influenced by forms of journalism open to user contributions; social media are used by institutions and movements as part of today's political debates and clashes. This has boosted a reshaping of the public sphere. But the democratization rhetoric that has surrounded these changes should not stop us from assessing the problems and questions that arise from the political significance of digital media. With new technologies, new forms of surveillance, censorship, and social control emerge. This may strengthen rather than weaken existing powers. Finally, in Chapter 6 we analyze the political economy of digital media by presenting the economic models that support corporations in contemporary capitalist societies. The battle for economic power involves workers' rights and welfare systems, as well as the balance of economic and financial globalization. Work and consumption are not spared from these changes, as they have changed extensively with the emergence of new forms of digital labor, new classes of service workers, and practices that cross the boundaries between production and consumption. Persistent inequalities characterize this landscape at both the local and global level, and are linked to broader issues of uneven economic and social development. Across the book, chapters are supplemented by boxes that expand on specific topics or problems, such as intellectual property rights, gender and technology, the startup economy, and filter bubbles.

In sum, in what follows we focus on many of the social and political dimensions of digital media: their effects on information societies, the changes they have facilitated or caused, as well as the role of certain social groups, with their interests and values, in shaping today's digital technologies. We have attempted to approach this from a global perspective, as we discuss the emergence of new areas of digital media diffusion and innovation, particularly in Asia, as well as in emerging countries of the Global South. Our standpoint, however, is fundamentally Western. In addition, we strive to highlight the role of local cultures within the magma of digital communications. The lenses that we use to analyze digital media are also focused on how social factors, such as gender, race, or class, influence or are shaped by the use of technology and the distribution of power around it. In short, we try to deal critically with the visions and promises surrounding computers and networks in the information society, and to place them within the broader transformations of the economy, modes of production and consumption, politics, and social relations. To study digital media one must be able to account for the broader landscape in which they develop, and thus for the decisive role played by governments, corporations, and citizens. In turn, it would be impossible to understand the societies we live in without a deep knowl-edge of the social, political, and economic significance of digital tech-nologies. We hope that this book will help build the cultural and political skills that are necessary to understand these complex relations and fully take part in the future evolution of our information societies.

We wish to thank our colleagues in Italy and Canada for the advice, sug-gestions, and criticisms that have helped us shape this book. Finally, thank you to the students on our courses in Digital Media Studies at the University of Milan and Critical Analysis of Media at the University of Toronto Mississauga, who have experienced firsthand the evolution of this book.

Alessandro Delfanti
Adam Arvidsson

Part I

Frameworks

1

Media and Digital Technologies

Digital media have become part of everyday life. In order to understand the consequences of this, we need not only consider the technological features of digital media. We must also analyze the social, political, and economic contexts within which digital media have emerged. Technologies are not neutral, but have complex histories that weave together social, cultural, and political factors with technical and material possibilities. The social sciences have developed various approaches aimed at understanding the relation between technology and society, and the ways in which they influence each other and co-evolve.

1.1 The Digital Environment

Contemporary societies are marked by the omnipresence and pervasiveness of digital media. Through the mass diffusion of personal computers, smartphones, tablets and other mobile technologies, and an accompanying near-ubiquitous connectivity, in the last two decades digital media have entered into the daily life of ordinary people. Processes of mediatization, that is the increasing presence of media in all aspects of life, have pushed social theorists to propose that we live what Mark Deuze calls *media lives* (2012). The digital media environment that we live in is widespread, fluid, and highly efficient. Indeed we have come to take digital connectivity for granted. We only note its absence: when we are disconnected, it is stressful and problematic. Think of when your phone stops working as the train you are riding goes into a tunnel. Furthermore, the billions of microprocessors and computers diffused worldwide are used in a wide range of human activities, from agriculture to industrial production, services, entertainment, and education. Overall,

Introduction to Digital Media, First Edition. Alessandro Delfanti and Adam Arvidsson.
© 2019 John Wiley & Sons, Inc. Published 2019 by John Wiley & Sons, Inc.

the transformations introduced by digital technologies are changing the ways in which we produce and distribute information and knowledge, as well as the ways in which we work and socialize. Mediatization is indeed a process with far-reaching consequences. On the one hand, as media studies scholars Nick Couldry and Andreas Hepp put it, the term refers to "the increasing temporal, spatial and social spread of mediated communication": we are surrounded by more and more media technologies in all aspects of our lives, in many different contexts, and across time and space. On the other, the concept stresses "the social and cultural differences that mediated communications make at higher levels of organizational complexity," which means that the outcome of such processes goes far beyond human communication and invests all human relations (2017, p. 35). In sum, digital media have become so pervasive that the changes, challenges, and opportunities that they bring along assume a ubiquitous reach. Media theorist Felix Stalder describes this as the "digital condition," a state in which computer networks have become "the key infrastructure for virtually all aspects of life" (2018, p. vii). This deep shift means that we now need to rethink the significance of terms like "democracy," "participation," "work," "property," and "power" in the light of the transformations linked to the emergence of digital technologies.

The evolution of computers is part of the history of the information society, which began centuries ago with the idea that information about social and economic facts could be collected, stored, and calculated. But the history of the electronic computers and computer networks that constitute digital media goes back several decades too (see Sections 2.4 and 2.5). Yet some recent events were crucial to give shape to the internet and computers we know today. The spread of digital media has grown steadily since the 1980s. Since then, we have seen the diffusion of (relatively) cheap and easy-to-use personal computers, themselves an effect of the evolution of microprocessor technology. The introduction of the World Wide Web in the 1990s brought internet connectivity into most homes and businesses in the advanced economies. The 2000s gave us the collaborative web: software and online platforms that allow all users to produce and distribute digital content. More recently, mobile technologies such as smartphones and tablets have transformed the daily experience of the internet, further integrating digital media into the flow of everyday life. In 2018, in the US, Canada, Italy, and many other Western countries, about 90% of the population use the internet on a daily basis, and almost as many own a smartphone. Globally, the number of internet users has passed four billion, or more than half of the world's population. The spread of digital media has been explosive. From 2000 to 2018 internet users increased 10-fold, and the massive spread of smartphones and internet use in areas like Asia, Africa, and South America in the last decade has changed the geography of the information society. China alone has 700 million internet users, and the rate of penetration has recently passed 50%. This challenges established assumptions about development and is rearranging the global role of some countries and areas of the world.[1]

The emergence and success of technologies that process information in digital formats have brought about profound changes in the way the media works. Thanks to the ability to integrate and interact with most other existing technologies, digital media have assumed a key role in the organization of communication and information flows. These changes have an impact on the overall *ecology* of the media. According to this metaphor, new life-forms like search engines, social networks, and mobile phone operators grow and prosper. They thrive on new survival strategies. For example, social media provide free services in exchange of user data. At the same time, older organisms adapt and change within this new ecology. Newspapers use social media to distribute their content and compete for reader attention. Political parties use the internet to experiment with new communication strategies. Governments exploit their power over digital infrastructures to enact new forms of censorship and social control. Law scholar Yochai Benkler (2006) has suggested that we have witnessed the birth of a new digital environment. This environment is marked by new possibilities, challenges, conflicts, and controversies. Among those there are issues related to copyright, ownership, and management of the technological infrastructure of the internet, organization of work, freedom of information and censorship, and social and political participation. The increasingly central role of digital media in the ecology of information and communication has made them an important political and economic battleground. In today's society, digital technologies come to mediate social relationships and are crucial to the construction of individual identities. The emergence of a digital public sphere, in the form of a multitude of platforms and practices that enable masses of people to collaborate in the creation of content and information, is a phenomenon with implications that go far beyond technology. This has inspired radically diverse visions of the future that this book will explore in the coming chapters. The rest of this chapter discusses the cycles of evolution of media, and lays the ground for an analysis of the socio-technical characteristics of digital media, including their infrastructural features. Finally, the last section provides an overview of some of the most important theories of the relation between technology and society.

1.2   New and Old Media

In early scholarship about the rise of digital media, the definition "new media" was used to describe information and communication technologies based on digital code. "New media" signified the set of media technologies that had emerged since the last decades of the twentieth century. This distinguished them from "old media," which was a definition used to identify traditional mass media like television, newspapers, or radio. While stressing such difference, one of the most influential theorists of the time, Lev Manovich, described new media not only in terms of their underlying technologies, but also through an analysis of their aesthetics, cultures, and media practices: their "language" (2001). Doing so allowed him to discuss the emergence of computer-based media as part of a long cultural and technological history which involves expressive forms such as cinema, press, or visual art, while stressing the new possibilities offered by digital media. Almost 20 years later, today's media studies scholarship would see equating digital media and "new media" as problematic in many ways. To be sure, digital media have certain common characteristics that distinguish them from analog media (see Section 1.3). Yet media that have emerged in the last 40 years or so are based on heterogeneous computing technologies and are very different from each other. Think of the radical difference between two digital technologies such as GPS navigators and digital cameras. Furthermore, digital computers have by now been around for many decades. They are not really "new" anymore. The term "new" also implied a linear view of the evolution of the media, which can lead people to overlook the context in which they emerge and think that they are somehow better than the "old" ones. Conversely, old media are sometimes held to be better than new media, as older technologies can be represented as more authentic. For example, many claim to have a deeper relationship with books than with e-books, or with vinyl records than with MP3 files.

Yet this does not mean that the difference between old and new media is uninteresting. For example, when studying media evolution, we must acknowledge that all media are "new" when they have just been introduced. The press is a dated technology by now, but at the time of its introduction it had a revolutionary impact on the transformation of modern societies. And yet today we tend to think of the press as a taken-for-granted "old" media technology. The notion of newness also usually entails certain visions of the future in which the "new" media play a key part. These visions can be hopeful or bleak. This has happened throughout history. It happened with the novel, with the telegraph, with movies, and with television. To some extent, such new media have changed the way in which people go about their everyday life, but often the hopes (or fears) attached to them turn out to be exaggerated. Finally, when new media are introduced they do not replace old media, but rather integrate or change them. The introduction of television has not caused the disappearance of the newspaper. The introduction of the tablet did not cause the disappearance of the book. Rather, books evolved into different technological formats. This process of evolution, called *remediation*, entails competition as well as coevolution and cooperation among different media (Bolter and Grusin 2000). A practice, content, or format can be re-mediated by a new technology that mimics or reworks previous formats. For example, the design of some web radio receivers reproduces 1950s radio sets. Wikipedia mirrors and is structured like a traditional encyclopedia, so that cross-references between entries allow a non-linear reading path, although this is made possible via hyperlinking technologies rather than by manually turning the pages. Some social media look like the cut-and-paste fanzines of the 1980s, produced with scissors and Xerox copiers. After all, even the first printed books of early modern Europe resembled manuscripts. In turn, the e-book is technologically very different from the printed book, but readers will immediately recognize the common genealogy, anchored in common features like the pages, cover, or table of contents, which make the reading experience similar. Overall new media do not come out of nowhere, but rather evolve from existing practices and media technologies. The concept of remediation allows the recognition that the history of media is a continuous, non-linear process that can go in several directions, as old and new media continue to influence each other. For example, newer formats can provide content and aesthetics that are adapted in older formats: *Assassin's Creed* is a franchise based on a video game but its stories are expanded to a broader set of media, such as films, comic books, and novels (Veugen 2016).

If instead of individual media we focus on the more general aspect of the continuing development of communication technologies, novelty becomes an important factor. In fact, part of the experience of digital media lies in the continuous succession of rapid technological cycles that bring new gadgets, new applications, and new services to the market. This is important because the early stages of life of an emerging media technology are characterized by uncertainty about its role. New media are not immediately accepted as natural components of the social world, and their meaning is initially open and contested. This phase has been defined as the "identity crisis" of new media (Gitelman and Pingree 2003). After its introduction, the meanings and functions of a new technology are slowly shaped by existing patterns of media usage and by the habits and desires of new users, as well as by technological characteristics. For example, new media such as the telephone in the mid-twentieth century or image messaging technologies in the early twenty-first century have both been met with anxieties about their role in the life of teenagers (see Section 3.6). The phase of crisis and novelty is resolved when a new technology becomes a mass consumer product. In a process of "domestication," the new technology is accepted in a society, it becomes everyday and understandable and tends not to cause rejection or fear anymore (Pantzar 1997).

If all old media were new at some point in their evolution, it is also true that sooner or later all new media are destined to grow old, fall behind, or be superseded by newer technologies. Some media may be abandoned, as happened to the phonograph or the telegraph. Some can even disappear and be forgotten, as the zograscope, an eighteenth-century device that used a lens to artificially provide depth to two-dimensional images; it now survives only in museums. However, often times media that seem to have disappeared leave traces behind, or are updated onto new media formats and technologies. Contemporary 3D media are indebted to a series of previous technologies, from the zograscope to the red and cyan glasses used to obtain anaglyph stereoscopic effects. In other cases, a medium can instead survive in niche markets or at least partially come back into fashion, like vinyl records in the 2010s. Many old media can be seen as "undead": their imminent death is announced or assumed but they refuse to disappear. This is the case of the printed book, which was thought to be doomed by the emergence of e-books, or the analog radio, which was to be killed by podcast and streaming technologies. Instead, both have experienced a resurgence in the last few years. Finally, abandoned media can be brought back to life by users who attach new meanings to them, somewhat making them "new" again: we could call these "zombie media." Media archeology studies once forgotten technologies, analyzing how they fell into disuse and how they are revitalized, often by means of artistic practices or user reappropriation (Parikka 2013). For example, the Gameboy, a portable video game console produced by Nintendo which had widespread commercial success in the 1990s, is now used to produce "8bit" techno music through do-it-yourself musical software.

1.3 Digital Media

While it is important to acknowledge that they are not completely different from older media forms and technologies, one of the defining technological characteristics of contemporary media technologies is that they are digital. This core technological feature brings with it a number of other key characteristics that distinguish them from analog media. In turn, these features are critical to understanding the ways in which digital media impact overall social dynamics, as well as economic and political relations. This book adopts a broad definition of media, as it includes many technologies that share the ability to mediate human activities, even beyond communication practices. Personal computers, mobile phones and smartphones, tablets, digital cameras, video game consoles, telecommunications satellites, credit cards, MP3 players, RFID (radio frequency identification) chips, televisions, servers, browsers, social media services, or self-tracking gadgets are all based on the processing of information in digital formats. This means that they carry information represented by a numeric code and then transform it into human language. This code is "digital" in the sense that it is based on the binary distinction between two symbols, 1 and 0. Analog media instead rely on continuous scales, like the scale of colors that can be represented by the chemical composition of a piece of celluloid film, or the letters of the alphabet that can be rearranged into words and expressions. Thanks to their binary code, digital media can carry information very efficiently and, most importantly, they can transform any analog code into their own binary language. For example, a digital camera converts an analog signal (the light entering the lens) into a digital code (the file in which the image is stored in the camera). Conversely, an MP3 player transforms a digital code (the MP3 file) into an analog signal (the music that streams to the speakers or headphones).

Yet in order to lay the ground for an understanding of the social implications of these set of technologies, we need to go beyond these mere technical aspects. Building upon a number of media theorists, we propose a list of some of the defining features of digital media: they are of course digital, but also convergent, hypertextual, distributed, pervasive, algorithmic, asymmetric, and both ephemeral and permanent.

1.3.1 Convergent

On digital media, different types of content (written, audio, visual, etc.) converge onto a single technical platform. The personal computer, for example, is at the same time a television set, a typewriter, a radio, a telephone, and countless other machines. Thanks to the digitization of information, computers are "universal machines" that can mimic other machines. This means that the production and consumption of different kinds of media content (film, text, music, etc.) no longer presupposes different kinds of hardware (projectors, books, stereos) that use different codes and technological supports (celluloid, paper, vinyl), but can happen on a set of machines, such as computers, digital cameras, or smartphones, where all these different kinds of content are represented by means of the same binary code. This goes beyond the technical level and implies a cultural convergence between producers and consumers of media content (Jenkins 2006).

1.3.2 Hypertextual

A hypertext is a text that embodies references to other texts or other forms of content. On the World Wide Web, hypertexts are a fundamental feature that link one webpage to another. This way, digital media allow users to enjoy content in a non-linear fashion. On a webpage you do not have to read contents in a linear way, as you would with a book. Instead you can customize your reading experience, jumping from one text to another, to a video, to a Wikipedia entry, and then back to another webpage or app (Manovich 2001).

1.3.3 Distributed

Traditional mass media are centralized and unidirectional: information is transmitted from a central facility, such as a newsroom, to a large audience of readers. Digital media are instead characterized by a distributed model. Indeed the internet is composed by thousands of interconnected nodes rather than a few core hubs (see Section 1.4). Furthermore, the spread of cheap computers, tablets, and smartphones, along with widespread internet connectivity and software that foster the production of user-generated content, has allowed users to take a greater role in the creation of content. The resources for information production and distribution are at least partially in the hands of individuals who communicate horizontally via media platforms (Benkler 2006).

1.3.4 Pervasive

Mobile technologies, such as mobile phones, smartphones, and tablets, give a pervasive or even ubiquitous scope to digital media (Deuze 2012). In fact they allow people to access and post information at any time and from any location, and companies to track and surveil user behavior at an unprecedented scale. This makes it possible to produce and exchange information specifically related to the place and time of use: to upload information on a shared map, for example Google Maps, or to communicate and interact with those who are attending an event in a particular location, for example textually via Twitter or with a video via Periscope. Mobile technologies have the ability to modify and extend our social networks. In this sense, they are not only a means for creating abstract communities, but also a tool to strengthen social ties connected to specific physical locations or territories.

1.3.5 Algorithmic

Most digital media services and technologies are underpinned by algorithms. These are programs that follow procedural logics in order to generate specific outputs. The role of algorithms is made possible by the fact that digital technologies "datafy" behaviors and interactions, or transform them into data that can be analyzed and then used to make choices. Algorithms bring with them a promise of objectivity, as they are supposed to be accurate and free from bias or external influence (Gillespie 2014). And yet the study of their logics and effects has found that, like any human technology, they are not neutral (see Box 3.2). The term "algocracy" describes situations in which power is exercised by algorithms that affect action by making some kinds of interaction or organization possible and blocking others (Aneesh 2009). For example, Facebook's algorithms analyze the activities of users and estimate which content is more likely to generate interactions if shown on their timeline. Software, in sum, structures all activities mediated by digital technologies. Many algorithms are based on machine learning technologies. This means that while using a certain service, individuals contribute to training algorithms.

1.3.6 Asymmetric

Digital media are highly commodified, as the biggest services are owned by a handful of gigantic corporations. In this landscape, power is unevenly distributed, as individual users do not have access to the information these corporations collect about their interactions and behaviors, although such information shapes the way users interact with a certain platform or service (Rosenblat and Stark 2016). Users do not know the algorithms that underpin the functioning of Tinder, and need to guess how to influence the way the platform decides to which other users one's profile will be suggested as a possible match. Indeed digital media tend to be perceived as black boxes that obscure the underlying operations that structure user experience. In many cases, users do not receive any economic benefit from their participation in such services. Finally, digital media are subject to pervasive surveillance and can be used for social and political control (Zuboff 2016).

1.3.7 Ephemeral or Permanent?

Different media have different duration and persistence. The paper book can be stored for centuries; inscriptions on stone last for millennia. In the case of the information produced and transmitted by digital media, its duration in time depends on several factors. The hard disks used to store data in digital form tend not to last more than one or two decades. The softwares that transform human language into binary code are quickly replaced by new programs. At a stage of human history in which knowledge is archived and stored on digital media, these problems assume a central importance for institutions like libraries or archives, whose mandate includes the preservation of documents for future generations. At a different level, digital communications like messages, chats, or pictures are perceived as being highly ephemeral (Grainge 2012). However, copies and traces of these communications can be duplicated and stored for years without the author's knowledge, by the companies that manage digital communication services, by government agencies, or by other individuals.

Box 1.1 The Materiality of Digital Media

The digitization of information and media content has not made the "stuff" of technology disappear. Digital materialism is a recent object of study for the social sciences (Casemajor 2015), which have been paying renewed attention to the physical characteristics of computer and network technologies, such as cables, microprocessors, routers, or towers for mobile telephony. Studying the materiality of media makes it possible to analyze the movement of so-called digital artifacts, the objects made of bytes that make up the content of digital technologies. Furthermore, paying attention to the materiality of digital technologies permits focus on the working conditions and the ecological aspects that make the media system possible. Manufacturing, transporting, and marketing digital goods is a global enterprise that mobilizes millions of workers and makes use of a large amount of raw materials and natural resources.

The ecological impact of digital technologies is often overlooked or ignored. Computers, tablets, game consoles, cellphones, and other digital technologies contain raw materials that require large energy resources to be mined and processed, and leave behind a trail of ecological degradation (Cubitt 2016). Digital technologies have given rise to an industry of recycling that extracts precious metals from decommissioned objects and sells them back to manufacturers. However this phase is also polluting, as it produces toxic wastes and consumes a large amount of energy. The digital industry mobilizes natural resources on a global scale, from raw materials extracted in Africa or South America, via the gigantic factories that assemble digital gadgets in Asia, up to end-users around the world, and then back to landfills, often in poor countries. For example, ore minerals like neodymium or coltan provide essential components for computers and smartphones and are often mined in African countries or in China, with environmental and labor standards well below those of Western countries. Planned obsolescence is a widespread practice that contributes to such request for resources. Computers and other commercial products are designed to have an artificially short lifespan, thus creating a continuous demand for raw materials (Rivera and Lallmahomed 2016). There is also a cultural obsolescence, as the continuous marketization of new models, for example of iPhones, pushes consumers to replace functioning phones in order to catch up with innovation cycles.

While charging a computer or a smartphone does not involve a large consumption of electricity, the data centers that store and distribute the information that we produce or download are important consumers of energy, in particular for cooling the processors. According to estimates produced by Greenpeace, internet infrastructures consume around 7% of global electricity and produce a substantial fraction of global CO_2 emissions. The growth of energy consumption is due mainly to the popularity of particularly energy-intensive services, like video streaming, which represents almost 70% of internet traffic. On the other hand, major internet companies are taking steps to transition toward renewable energy (Greenpeace 2017).

1.4 Infrastructures and Platforms

The technical characteristics that underpin digital media reach global significance through the infrastructures that compose digital networks. Understanding the architecture and design of the "plumbing" of digital media is crucial for the study of the actors and communities that populate them (Musiani 2012). According to the American law scholar Lawrence Lessig (2002), "code is law." With this formula, Lessig suggested that the architecture of the different layers of digital networks is not neutral, but rather has the power to shape the behaviors of their users. As described in the next section, this is true of all technologies. Yet digital media are characterized by a set of specific and distinctive features. Unlike broadcast media, such as a television station or a newspaper, the internet is a communication system that is not based on a single central hub. Instead it is composed by a series of interconnected nodes. Indeed the internet is a distributed structure shaped as a network, which means that information is physically located on thousands of computers called servers, to which other computers connect to request the information they want, such as that making up a website. The shutdown of a server does not shut down the network as a whole, but only makes the specific information contained there inaccessible. The internet is also a redundant network: information is disassembled into packets that can separate and travel on many different paths. Therefore, the interruption of a specific communication line does not affect their transfer. Furthermore, the internet is an open system: anyone with access to a telephone or broadband line can access it, either with a personal computer or another device. Anyone can create a new server. The standards and the languages used to transfer information on the web are open and available to anyone who wants to use them.

These infrastructural features are based upon a global governance system (Mueller 2010). The World Wide Web Consortium (W3C) is an international organization that deals with web standards, with the task of keeping them open. Each website has an "address" where it can be reached, that is, an alphanumeric code that identifies the site and allows users to get to the server on which the information that constitutes it is stored. These codes are called domains and are managed and awarded by an international organization, the Internet Corporation for Assigned Names and Numbers (Icann). There are national domains, such as .it, .ca, or .se, or others that define the type of activity carried out by the site, such as .com for commercial activities or .org for associations and non-profit organizations. The circulation of information is based on the principle of network neutrality. This means that internet providers cannot discriminate information packets according to the content or origin. Companies that produce content cannot pay providers to pass their information more quickly: the download speed of a site relative to another depends on the source from which it is downloaded and not by the provider's decision to assign it a privileged status. This principle is constantly under attack by connectivity providers who could generate greater profits by charging fees for the privileged treatment of some information providers (see Box 4.3). For example, major corporations such as Netflix would be willing to pay internet providers to speed up their content at the expense of other websites.

To understand digital media it is important to differentiate the levels that compose them. As argued by Yochai Benkler, digital media and network technologies are composed of different "layers," that are related to one another but have their own peculiarities, problems, and challenges (2006). The first is the physical layer: It is composed of material components such as the frequencies that are used for radio broadcasts, and the cables, computers and servers, satellites, and telephone lines that make up the internet. The second is the logical layer, composed of the software, standards, and protocols that underpin digital networks: For example, the TCP/IP protocols that allow for the transfer of information on the internet, or the software that manages an online platform, social network, or database. The third is the content layer, that is, the humanly intelligible information that is produced and exchanged within the network: for example, the text of an article in an online newspaper, the content of an email, or a picture posted on a social media. Finally, there is also the legal layer, the set of national and international laws and policies governing the functioning of digital networks and the behavior of their users. This level is related to the other three.

Another important focus of studies of digital media is represented by one component of digital media infrastructures: *platforms*. From a technical viewpoint, a digital platform is nothing else than a software environment in which a set of programs can be executed. In this sense both a browser such as Firefox or an operating system such as Android can be seen as platforms, as they are environments for other applications – think of a Netflix movie watched on Firefox, or an app downloaded onto an Android phone. Media scholars researching social media platforms have analyzed the way these services use algorithms to organize and mediate the interactions that are carried out through their interfaces. For example, Tinder is a platform that organizes the search for romantic and sexual relationships by analyzing and coding user preferences; Instagram uses the same principles to mediate the circulation and exchange of images. In this sense, platforms are stages that allow users to perform specific activities (Gillespie 2010) while shaping how such activities can be carried out. Studying platforms requires going beyond an analysis of their software. Media theorist José van Dijck (2013b) has proposed that we look at platforms both as cultural constructs, thus highlighting the way they shape sociality and cultural production (see Chapter 3), and economic structures, therefore focusing on problems of ownership and business models (see Chapter 6). Theories of the relation between technology and society can help understand how these phenomena unfold.

1.5   Technology and Society

The social sciences, like sociology and anthropology, have developed theories that allow for an in-depth analysis of the link between technology, media, and society. These can help us develop a critical view on the role and evolution of digital media. Indeed, the social sciences aim at questioning widespread views and common sense in order to arrive at more deeply documented theories that take the complexity of social phenomena into account. The most important theories of the relation between technology and society have developed from the study of the technologies that were predominant in the twentieth century (Sismondo 2011). The emergence of digital technologies poses new challenges that oblige us to rethink and renew these approaches. Yet these critical tools remain essential to studying the relation between technology and its social and political contexts.

Some theories of the relation between technology and society see technology as an exogenous factor, that is, an external force that develops independently of social phenomena. Here the important thing is not so much how a particular technology has developed, but what function it performs in relation to a society. In this view, computers are functional to the aims of the institutions or social groups that use them. A similar approach is *technological determinism*, which understands technology as an independent force that can determine the development of a society. From this perspective, the characteristics of digital media affect the way in which individuals interact with each other, giving rise to particular forms of social organization. They are also seen as responsible for changes in economic structures or business models. Some form of technological determinism is widespread in common-sense accounts, such as policy initiatives relating to digital technologies or journalism describing the changes that they bring about. For example, it has been common for some time to attribute the upheavals of the 2011 "Arab Spring" to the spread of social media technologies like Facebook and Twitter (see Box 5.2). More or less pronounced versions of technological determinism can be found also in social theory. For Karl Marx, technologies and relations of production are strictly intertwined. Trivializing his vision, we could say that the steam engine was an important factor that contributed to the emergence of an industrial capitalist society. Similar positions were taken by more recent media scholars. According to Marshall McLuhan's famous motto, "the medium is the message." McLuhan, perhaps the most influential media theorist of the 1960s, thought that the "media form" of communication technologies used in any given society had a decisive impact on its development, regardless of the content of the communications, that is, the message they transmitted. One of his most famous books, *Understanding Media*, opens by stating that "the personal and social consequences of any medium – that is, of any extension of ourselves – result from the new scale that is introduced into our affairs […] by any new technology" (1964, p. 1). To simplify this position, we could say that the most important factor is not what is transmitted on television, but that the technology of television itself has been introduced into people's life, therefore allowing the transmission of moving image and sound regardless of space and time bounds. The determinist perspective remains one of the main ways used to interpret the social and economic dimension of digital media. It would be simplistic to think that new technologies do not have an impact in and by themselves: inventions like the wheel or means of communicating across distances, like the telegraph, have influenced deeply the development of human societies. However this view is too one-dimensional. It does not take adequate account of complexities that mark the relationship between technology and society. For example, technologies are often used in a different way and for different purposes by different social actors. The technological determinist approach, however, can be tempered by recognizing that, with their values and choices, individuals and social groups help to determine the role played by technology.

An opposite perspective is *social construction of technology*. This theoretical approach suggests that the development, structure, and significance of a technology depends on the strength, needs, and values of the social groups that promote and design it (Bijker 1997). The construction metaphor implies that the evolution of a technology is something in which people participate actively. This approach emphasizes how the design and meaning of technologies depend on the social processes from which they originate and by which their development is shaped. According to this perspective, the open and distributed architecture of the internet is not emerging from a vacuum, but rather due to the values and choices of the scientists and engineers who have designed its network structure and standards. For example, the political choices of programmers and hackers belonging to the counterculture of the 1970s and 1980s, influenced the decision, again by scientists, to release the standards and codes on which the web runs as open formats, so that anyone could use and improve them. Other actors would have built a network different from that which we know today. Indeed, according to the definition of Science and Technology Studies theorist Langdon Winner (1980), technologies are not neutral but rather have a "politics." The way they are designed or the decision to adopt them in different contexts might strengthen the agenda of a particular group. This approach leads to the question of why a certain technology has assumed a certain form instead of another, what are the actors who have contributed to its development and evolution, and why it has been chosen over competitive technologies. Others have focused on the "bias" that certain actors can build into a certain technological system (Friedman and Nissembaum 1997). For example, as the values of the engineers who design an algorithm play a role in their technical choices, this algorithm can reflect such values by favoring or discriminating against certain individuals or groups (see Box 3.2). Similar approaches also recognize the active role of users of technologies. Often early adopters or new users of a new technology develop practices that were never intended by the people who designed and commercialized it, or assign new meanings to a certain technology and thus contribute to shaping it.

Box 1.2 Users Matter

In studies of the relation between technology and society, the user is a crucial object of research. Indeed the user represents the human factor interacting with the machine, and must not be overlooked: "users matter," to use the title of one of the most important books on the subject (Oudshoorn and Pinch 2003). In this perspective, consumption is a complex cultural activity not only related to purchasing, but also to how users repurpose, modify, and resist technology.

On the one hand, the design of technologies has the power to "configure" users (Woolgar 1990). For example, the lack of interoperability of the software and standards of an Apple laptop pushes its users to interact only with gadgets and services commercialized by the same company, such as iPhones, iPads, or iTunes. This constrains and guides the user's online behavior. In turn, users are not just passively configured by technologies, and can contribute to shaping digital media in ways that often go beyond those imagined by those who designed and programmed a specific platform. One example of this is the practice of jailbreaking, that is, the removal of limitations built into a computer system, for example Apple's iOS operating system that runs Apple products. Thanks to software tools that provide access to the operating system, these practices allow users to install applications that are not officially provided by the manufacturer (Magaudda 2010). Users' power to reconfigure digital media also has to do with the degree to which technologies are open to tinkering and transformative interventions. Technologies are indeed marked by different levels of openness (see Chapter 4). They can be designed to be accessible and easily transformable, or may have blocks or obstacles that prevent users from changing a system or using it for unintended purposes, as is the case with Apple products.

Scholars have also noted the existence of "superusers" with specific technical skills and professional positions. In the case of digital media, these would be figures such as software engineers, system administrators (sys-admins), or hackers (Brunton and Coleman 2014). As they design and maintain digital networks and algorithms, these users occupy a privileged position. Their cultures and practices are thus particularly interesting for the study of digital technologies. Finally, non-users also matter: the individuals who resist or reject technologies tend to be invisible to scholars who study digital media, but their motivations and choices can shed light on the relation between technology and society (Wyatt et al. 2003). For example, deciding not to participate in social media communication can be a form of resistance to the widespread corporate surveillance carried on within such platforms (see Box 5.3).

Finally, some social theories speak of the *co-production of technology and society*. In this framework, both the above perspectives, which state that social forces shape technologies or that technologies determine social development, are seen as limited. Rather, society and technology influence and shape each other in a process of coevolution where one level continuously influences the development of the other, and vice-versa (Jasanoff 2004). These, and other, theoretical approaches are updated and adapted to the study of digital media and their specific characteristics. For example, sociologists use the term *affordances*, borrowed from design and engineering, to describe how technologies both enable and limit what users can do with them. As Donald Norman put it, "affordances specify the range of possible activities" (1999). New technologies can provide solutions and enable new forms of action, but at the same time this is only possible within the boundaries of the technology itself. Platforms like Twitter or wiki softwares are enabling technologies that allow users to create certain types of actions within specific limits. Twitter allows temporary publics to join an event and follow and comment on it. But at the same time this needs to be done within a format of messages that does not exceed a certain number of characters. This way, Twitter drives users to follow an established pattern that derives from the constraints imposed by the platform.

Note

1 For up-to-date data on the spread and use of digital networks see the Internet World Stats, www.internetworldstats.com.

2

The Information Society

The history of computers is linked to the history of the idea that it is possible to apply a scientific method to human affairs. The production and management of information have assumed a key role in advanced societies, and have led to the emergence of terms such as "information society." The increasingly central position of information in social, political, and economic evolution has been made possible thanks to the evolution of computers and networks, as well as the contributions of many different social actors. The information society is not a given, but rather a project that continues to grow in new directions.

2.1   A New Society?

The concept of *information society* refers to a form of society characterized by the importance of the production and management of information and knowledge (Webster 2014). In information societies, technologies for the production, manipulation, and communication of information are pervasive and affect social and productive processes, as well as personal and political identities. The ability to produce, manipulate, and distribute information becomes one of the main factors related to wealth and power, and therefore a battleground of economic, social, and political development for individuals, businesses, and governments. The birth and affirmation of the information society are not only related to the spread of digital information and communication technologies, but also to the economic and political upheavals of the last few decades of the twentieth century, such as the end of the bipolar world, as well as the emergence of globalization processes and new production paradigms. Since the early 1960s these changes have been described with definitions that, while adopting different vantage points, tend to refer to the same set of phenomena. For example,

Introduction to Digital Media, First Edition. Alessandro Delfanti and Adam Arvidsson.
© 2019 John Wiley & Sons, Inc. Published 2019 by John Wiley & Sons, Inc.

the second half of the twentieth century saw the emergence of concepts such as "post-industrial society," "post-modern society," "post-Fordism," "knowledge society," "network society," and "cognitive capitalism" (Kumar 1995). Underlying these descriptions is the shared awareness of a historic break with previous forms of production and social organization. Under this new paradigm, information and knowledge became key inputs in the economy and organization of contemporary societies. The technologies which are used to produce, manage, and distribute information are widespread and characterized by decreasing costs, at least in rich countries where increasingly large sections of the population have access to a computer connected to digital networks and companies can organize their production processes and business through information technologies. In addition, information technologies make social and productive structures more flexible, as they allow actors to organize and carry out networked processes that would have been too costly and inefficient under traditional forms of organization.

The concept of "information society" began to spread in the 1990s, both in the public debate and within academia. The spread of the internet, which accelerated in the second half of the decade, created a feeling of radical change. Visions of economic transformation were boosted by hopes about the democratic and transparent nature of new technologies, as well as their wide social effects. According to this "cyber-utopian" view (Morozov 2011), digital networks would lead to widespread access to knowledge and a radical political democratization, as well as to a new economy based on communication and flexibility. In the economic realm, the birth of the information society was described as a third industrial revolution (Rifkin 2011): if the first was that of the steam engine and the second that of electricity and the internal combustion engine, the third would be based on technologies for the production, management, and transmission of information. This does not mean that change is limited to the growth of the tertiary sector. Information technologies are changing deeply even the agricultural and industrial sectors. Indeed specific technologies converge into integrated systems in which they become indistinguishable: computers are necessary for operating a factory, for managing a network of suppliers, for DNA sequencing, as well as for the sale of consumer products. Over the last two centuries, the industrial revolution has changed farming by introducing agricultural machinery, chemical fertilizers, and new systems of food transformation and distribution. Similarly, the information revolution is transforming industry (think of robots working in an assembly line or the online purchase of industrial goods) and agriculture (think of engineered genetically modified organisms or weather forecasts based on satellites and predictive software).

2.2   The Networked Economy and Globalization

The debate on the rise of the information society has been dominated by the figure of the Catalan sociologist Manuel Castells, who in the 1990s articulated a detailed account of what he saw as a new era in the evolution of contemporary society, with effects in economy and politics (Stalder 2006). Castells's thesis contains a certain amount of technological determinism. In fact he formalized the economic, social, and political role of information in a changing society. In industrial societies, economic and political power was linked to the production of material objects. In information societies, informational or intangible assets such as brands, innovation, and knowledge determine economic success. The era of informational capitalism begins. Moreover, Castells described networks as the core organizational structures. In fact, with the evolution of his work he tended to use the term "network society," as in the title of the first volume of his trilogy: *The Rise of the Network Society* (1996). The economic system that has emerged from this transformation is characterized by being, in Castells's definition, informational, global, and networked.

In the *informational economy*, productivity, competitiveness, and profitability depend on the ability to generate and manipulate information and knowledge. Research and development, and thus innovation, become crucial for the enterprise. Indeed in the 1970s the money spent by the private sector in scientific and technological research exceeded public investment for the first time since World War II, a trend that continues today. The main resources of the informational economy are not factories and machinery, but rather those related to information: brands, patents, the ability to manage networks of suppliers, subcontractors, and distributors, as well as design and marketing operations. Companies like Nike or Apple do not own the factories that produce their shoes or smartphones: the production of material goods is subcontracted to external producers, often in Asia. Western companies own the intellectual property (patents on product innovation and trademark rights), conduct research and development, organize networks of suppliers and sales operations, and manage marketing and communication. Controlling these informational goods is more profitable, given that the capital invested in information provides a higher return than that invested in material production. Information and knowledge are both the raw material and the output of the production processes these companies control. Further, information is an intangible good that is crucially different from material goods and needs to be regulated by specific forms of property. Thus in an information society intellectual property rights acquire unprecedented importance (Hesse 2002). For companies that produce goods with a high information content, such as in hi-tech or the cultural industry, owning patents or copyrights becomes crucial. In fact, since the early 1980s intellectual property rights have been expanded to the results of scientific research conducted in public universities, as well as to new types of informational goods. Intellectual property rights have become longer and are more closely integrated at the national and global level (see Box 2.1).

Box 2.1 Intellectual Property Rights

Intellectual property rights are an array of legal principles that enable creators and inventors to exercise ownership rights over the fruits of inventiveness and ingenuity. These rights grant a temporary monopoly on the exploitation of an intangible asset and permit the exclusion of third parties from its use. Intellectual property rights are divided in three main types:

- *Copyright* protects artistic, literary, and scientific work: for example, a song, a book, or a newspaper article;
- *Patents* protect industrial inventions: innovations that in addition to being new and original are reproducible and applicable to industrial activities. For example, a new microchip or touchscreen technology. However, in recent decades patents have also been expanded to discoveries such as genetic sequences.
- *Trademarks* distinguish a product or a company, making them recognizable by the consumer.

Intellectual property is a temporary concession that was originally meant to boost creative and inventive activities. After a certain period of time, works or inventions enter the public domain, so that all of society can benefit from them. This is based on the premise that information is different from material goods. Although both can be traded on the market, from an economic point of view a car is quite different from a song. First, a car is a material and tangible good that, if possessed by an individual, cannot be owned by another. Second, the cost of producing a car lowers as the number of pieces produced increases: for example, the cost of building an assembly line is spread over the thousands of cars it will produce over the years. But the cost of producing a material good never reaches zero. Instead, an intangible good such as a song behaves differently. Economists say that information is a non-rival good, and has a marginal cost of zero. Non-rival means that the fact that a person sings a song does not prevent others from doing the same at the same time: unlike in the case of cars, which cannot be used by two people at the same time, there is no rivalry among the users of a song. The marginal cost of reproducing information tends to be zero: recording a song has an initial cost, but the cost of producing copies is negligible. Digital technologies have accentuated this feature: today, producing a new copy of a movie in a computer is simple, fast, and virtually without costs. Intellectual property rights establish artificial marginal costs in the form of licensing fees to be paid to produce a copy of an intangible asset such as a copyrighted song or to build a patented machinery.

A *globalized economy* is characterized by economic institutions that have the organizational and technological capacity to operate on a global scale in real time. Globalization processes have been evolving for centuries: think of global areas of exchange and power such as the British Empire, or the transatlantic market in the nineteenth century, or the Italian maritime republics of the Middle Ages and the Renaissance (Stearns 2016). However, in today's information society globalization has become a major economic phenomenon underpinned by the emergence of new actors. Among the most important are organizations such as multinational companies, which use digital media and networks to control complex and transnational processes. Production, consumption, and movement of goods are thus organized on a global scale. This fosters the emergence of a global consumer culture in which goods, lifestyles, and forms of consumption spread around the world and are adapted in different local contexts. Think of hip hop music: born as a counterculture in urban black communities in the United States in the early 1980s, it was later imported to Europe, Africa, and Asia, giving rise to a plurality of musical styles associated with fashions and lifestyles that maintain a common origin. Global financial markets, which are managed through digital media and network technologies, are another feature of the globalized economy (see Section 6.4). Finally, the importance of supranational entities and treaties that include sets of countries or entire regions of the globe increases. This is the case of free trade agreements such as NAFTA (North American Free Trade Agreement), a treaty between Mexico, the United States, and Canada that has been in place since the 1990s, the European Union, the World Trade Organization, or the World Bank.

Finally, Castell's *networked economy* is characterized by flexible forms of production. The rigid hierarchies of factory work and the bureaucratic organizations of industrial society are transformed toward a new paradigm of the organization of production. The processes that underpin production in such a paradigm have been described as based on network structures, and thus organized around decentralized and autonomous production units. Networks of companies formed by suppliers, subcontractors, manufacturers, distribution companies, and commercial operations thrive in contemporary economies. This development is at least partially due to the impact of new information and communications technologies, which since the 1970s have made networks more efficient and competitive. Networks were not born with these changes, but rather are an archaic form of social organization: kinship networks are the fundamental form of tribal societies, and networks of business contacts by land and sea have been structuring globalization processes for centuries. Networks of more or less spontaneous cooperation among a multitude of small players without centralized decision hubs, such as street markets, have dominated production, distribution, and consumption of goods until the modern era. However, with the advent of industrial societies in the nineteenth century, the economies of scale based on centralized and bureaucratic organizations proved more efficient than existing networks and established themselves as the dominant form of economic organization. For example, large and centralized manufacturers of food and their distribution chains have taken over local economies, as they can move more and cheaper food to the market than small local producers with access to street markets. But with the emergence of the information society, networks have become competitive again. Information technologies enable the extremely efficient organization of actors that are not organized as a pyramidal hierarchy, but rather maintain partial autonomy of decision. Networks thus return to being an alternative to bureaucratic organizations (Castells 1996). For example, new food distribution networks such as food co-ops or food delivery platforms can coexist with the centralized systems that underpin large retailers.

According to Castells, as a result of their importance in the world of economic production, networks have become dominant also in the social dimension. He described a "space of flows" composed of the spaces, both physical and mediated, where information, money, and people circulate. This space is configured as an open network, in which national borders and boundaries among organizations, communities, and groups are becoming less important. In this space, a growing part of wealth is created through exchanges among people from different countries, organizations, or communities. Therefore, individuals who have access to the space of flows are the ones who possess the skills necessary to efficiently and productively exchange information or move freely in different places, or between one organization and another. These people can collaborate regardless of factors such as their ethnic or religious identity. At the other end of the spectrum, individuals who remain cut off from the space of flows do not have access to the internet or other channels that underpin flows of information and money, such as the financial market or transnational labor markets. They do not belong to the new class of knowledge workers who have a university education, are familiar with digital media, and have a cosmopolitan mindset based on a globalized consumer culture. For Castells, in information societies the main split is no longer linked only to the conflict between capital and workers, but rather expands to conflicts between those who have access to flows and those who are excluded from them. The latter tend to counteract the cosmopolitan and globalized culture of the space of flows by reinforcing their ethnic or cultural identities, which can become modes of resistance and opposition. Castells's examples of identity-based reactions to globalization were US far-right movements, Islamic fundamentalism, and the indigenous Zapatista rebellion of 1994 in Mexico. On the contrary, in the space of flows that dominate and drive the information society, conflicts are dampened and individuals compete freely for a success (or failure) which depends mainly on their ability to succeed as entrepreneurs.

2.3   Theories of the Information Society

Although he is probably the most influential, Castells is neither the only nor the first social theorist to describe the rise of an "information society" (Mattelart 2003). The term has a history that begins after World War II, when a number of Western scholars started proposing elements that would become central in Castells's vision, such as the weakening of the conflict between capital and labor and the new productive role of information flows. The history of these ideas is indeed characterized by some common elements. For example, technological determinism led many theorists to emphasize the effects of innovation on society. The first person to seriously investigate the new role of information and knowledge as crucial factors in advanced capitalist economies was the economist Fritz Machlup, who in the 1930s had begun to study the effect of patents on economic development. In the 1960s Machlup introduced and popularized the term "knowledge economy." Around the same time a major contemporary management thinker, Peter Drucker, pointed out how knowledge workers – researchers, managers, engineers, and technicians – were assuming a central role as the organizations of the capitalist economy became more complex and the source of value moved toward innovation and the organization of complex processes. Drucker (1957) was also one of the first to use the term "postmodern" to describe the model of society that was evolving around the new economic importance of information, and this was a term that was to become fashionable in the 1980s. The Marxist sociologist Daniel Bell (1973) expanded this vision of a new economic and social order, suggesting that the importance of the production and circulation of information as an economic factor, and thus the political and cultural centrality of knowledge workers, was rendering less influential the great ideologies of modernity, such as communism, which were organized around the conflict between capital and labor. In his opinion the new knowledge workers felt removed from the ideological views of the right or the left. Rather, as members of an emerging middle class, they were primarily interested in their role as consumers. Bell's argument resonated with broader debates of the postwar period, when the social sciences analyzed the spread of a new middle class with an apolitical and consumerist orientation, and economists argued that the antagonistic social models of United States and Soviet Union were destined to converge in a model dominated by the production of knowledge, structured in large and complex organizations, oriented toward economic growth and mass consumption, and less influenced by political ideologies.

Over the following decade, these ideas were consolidated and converged toward the concept of a new "postindustrial" society. Proposed by the sociologist Alain Touraine in 1971, and by Daniel Bell shortly after, the postindustrial society model was based on three main components. First, the reduction of the economic role of material industrial production and the consolidation of a new economy based on information and services. Second, the centrality of knowledge production, and in particular of scientific research, as the engine of economic and social development; Touraine included the industrialization of cultural production and its integration into the circuit of commodities. Third, the powerful role of the planning and organization of complex processes, and consequent replacement of the old ruling class with a class of bureaucrats and technicians who exercised power anonymously and apparently without political interests (Touraine 1971; Webster 2014).

Later, the theorists of "post-Fordism" put the emphasis on changes in the forms of production. The advent of computers and automated machines and tools instigated changes to the rigid and hierarchical organization of the Fordist factory to create more flexible forms of production (Tomaney 1994). Indeed, the organization of work based on the assembly line designed by Ford was perfect for producing standardized mass consumption goods, but in order to modify a product the entire production line had to be restructured. Instead, new machines such as robots were easily reconfigurable and could meet the demands of an ever-changing market. In the new factories even workers could be organized in teams rather than the traditional strictly pyramidal chain of command used in Fordist companies. The 1980s witnessed the re-emergence of the concept of postmodern society, an expression popularized by the French philosopher Jean-François Lyotard. His main argument was that the changes in the production of culture and knowledge, as well as political changes that have to do with the emergence of consumer cultures, would have a profound effect on contemporary societies. The grand narratives that had guided modern societies, such as faith in scientific rationality, social justice, and historic progress, would be supplanted by a relativism caused by the awareness of the artificial nature of human culture. In a postmodern society, overarching and cohesive worldviews such as those underpinned by the Enlightenment or Marxism would become irrelevant. According to Lyotard, when everything is reduced to information, everything can be revised, manipulated, modified, and commercialized, and nothing is stable. The Canadian media theorist Marshall McLuhan was one of the proponents of the role of new media as instruments of this kind of deep social change. McLuhan wrote in the 1960s, an era characterized by the mass diffusion of commercial television in Western countries. According to McLuhan, electronic media such as television were destined to transform humanity into a "global village," that is, a world shrunk by the ability to communicate in real time at a great distance provided by new media. Forms of face-to-face relationships that are typical of traditional societies would extend on a global scale. McLuhan not only advocated the liberation from centralized and bureaucratic societies whose emergence he attributed to printing technologies, but also the quenching of the differences between rich and poor countries, and the birth of a "global community" (1964). Yet his view was too nuanced to be described simply as utopian. For example, McLuhan warned against the societal turn fostered by electronic media and what he called the "tribal consequences" of the unification of human cultures in the global village (1962).

The spread of the internet in the mid-1990s provoked reactions and expectations similar to those developed with the arrival of the television or the popular press. A group of opinion leaders such as Kevin Kelly, Nicholas Negroponte, Stewart Brand, and Chris Anderson gathered around the magazine *Wired*, founded in 1993, and events such as TED conferences (Technology, Entertainment, and Design). They began to articulate a vision that derived from the culture that was already widespread within the entrepreneurial circles of Silicon Valley, located south of San Francisco in California. In particular Negroponte was painting digital networks as technologies that allow the spatial and bureaucratic barriers that characterize nation-states to be transcended (1995). In this vision, the individual is a consumer or an entrepreneur who lives in a space and market freed from the influence of the state. In some cases, these ideas assumed a more political perspective. For example, in 1996 the influential manifesto *A Declaration of the Independence of Cyberspace* described digital networks as free from government control and censorship: "We are creating a world where anyone, anywhere may express his or her beliefs, no matter how singular, without fear of being coerced into silence or conformity" (Barlow 1996). This wave of techno-libertarianism was later summarized in the formula "Californian Ideology," a denunciation of the view that the spread of the internet will lead to widespread access to knowledge and information and thus erase differences between consumers and producers, workers and employers, and state and citizens. This formula has been used to criticize the idea, widespread in Silicon Valley capitalism, according to which the free flow of information will bring about political democratization, while an economy based on "disruptive" hi-tech companies will open new possibilities for enrichment for those with the necessary flexibility and entrepreneurial spirit (Barbrook and Cameron 1996). Although the concept of a Californian Ideology seemed to exacerbate the internet's liberating potential, it also allowed the importance of radical movements and ideas in the development of the digital economy to be grasped. Adopting a social construction lens, one can focus on how specific groups linked to the evolution of digital media have been crucial actors in the evolution of contemporary digital technologies while infusing them with their political ideas and aspirations. For example, as we will see in the next section, by intervening in designing and repurposing computers and networks hacker communities can intervene in and redefine the political sphere (Coleman and Golub 2008). The expansion of such hacking practices outside the software world and toward fields such as biology or manufacturing can modify the social significance of technologies used in the life sciences or engineering (Delfanti 2013). These ideas have to do with cultural changes too. The very informational capitalism described by Castells has been said to be based on cultural foundations that are quite different from those of industrial capitalism. In the early 2000s Finnish philosopher Pekka Himanen, an author who has analyzed the cultural changes at the base of contemporary information societies, spoke explicitly of a new ethos of capitalism based on flexibility, creativity, and independence from hierarchies and industrial bureaucracies (2001). This position echoed those of authors who have updated Max Weber's ideas on the emergence of capitalism to describe a "new spirit of capitalism." According to such theories, contemporary societies co-opt and nurture cultural elements coming from social movements and adopt them as part of the culture of a flexible and consumerist capitalism (Boltanski and Chiappello 2007).

In the 1990s the idea of "collective intelligence" made inroads within media studies. According to the French philosopher Pierre Lévy, information technologies allow the mobilization and coordination of distributed intelligence (1997). Building upon Lévy's ideas, American media theorist Henry Jenkins described a media system in which people can share resources and combine skills thanks to a participatory culture of active and collaborative media production. Jenkins studied spoiler communities organized around reality television shows such as *Survivor*. He described how "through the mutual production and reciprocal exchange of knowledge" organized via community-based websites, these early online communities of fans were able to gather and share secret information about the show (2006). With a somewhat similar concept, that of "cognitive capitalism," a particular tradition of Marxist theorists focused on an analysis of the uneven relations of power between users and corporations. This form of capitalism is described as an organization of production based on the exploitation of the cognitive abilities of masses of individuals and made possible by the social characteristics of digital media. Indeed, in his work Karl Marx described the *general intellect* as the abstract scientific and tacit knowledge embedded in machines and based on social cooperation among workers. According to Marx, who was writing in the mid-nineteenth century, the general intellect was destined to become the main force of production in advanced societies. The information society has in a sense actualized Marx's prophecy, as the knowledge concentrated in information technologies has taken a leading role in today's economy. The theorists of cognitive capitalism pointed out that collective intelligence and social cooperation are exploited by capitalism, but can also constitute the possible bases of a new alternative (Moulier Boutang 2011; Hardt and Negri 2000). Social and political theorists have been chasing a new comprehensive definition to capture the economic transformations of capitalist societies in the age of ubiquitous digital media: for example, "digital capitalism" (see Section 6.1).

2.4 The History of Information Technologies

The evolution of the information society is closely related to the forms of information production and distribution that were established with the spread of computers first, and digital networks later. In turn, the history of information technologies cannot be separated from the great social and political changes of the last centuries. Indeed, calculating machines are the product of centuries of history. The abacus, the first machine to help individuals make calculations, was already being used by the Sumerians around 4500 years ago. However, the first definition of the computer as a machine equipped with the specific features that we attribute to it today comes from the English mathematician Alan Turing, who in the 1930s in his doctoral thesis theorized the computer as a machine "capable of imitating all other machines," that is, programmable toward different tasks (Agar 2017). Turing's definition captured the specificity of the computer vis-à-vis other technologies: a modern computer embodies a series of machines which previously lived separate lives: it is a typewriter, a DVD player, a phone, a camera, a calculator, a game console, a television.

Box 2.2 Timeline: the History of Computers

1673   *Germany*: Gottfried Leibniz invents the first mechanical calculator

1801   *France*: Joseph Marie Jacquard builds an automatic loom working according to a program stored in a perforated paper roll

1822   *Great Britain*: Charles Babbage designs the "difference engine" and in 1837 the "analytical engine." Neither is built during his lifetime

1843   *Great Britain*: Ada Lovelace publishes the article in which she describes Babbage's analytical engine as a programmable machine

1899   *United States*: the Hollerith tabulating machine is patented. It works with punched cards and is used in the following year's census. The company founded by Herman Hollerith goes on to become IBM

1931   *Great Britain*: Alan Turing defines the computer as a machine capable of imitating all other machines. According to the "Turing test," a machine is considered intelligent if a human being who interacts with it does not realize that they are interacting with a machine

1944   *United States*: the first electromechanical computer, the Mark I, is developed at Harvard. It weighs five tons, has a 72-bit RAM memory and a computing speed of 3 Hz

1944   *Great Britain*: Alan Turing's team develops the first fully electronic computer, Colossus, used to decrypt German military communications

1959   *United States*: the first electronic supercomputer, IBM Stretch, is sold to customers in the military–industrial complex, such as the US Navy, the French High Commission for Atomic Energy, and the Los Alamos scientific laboratories

1965   *Italy*: Olivetti launches the P101 or Perottina, named after its designer Pier Giorgio Perotto. Sold in tens of thousands of specimens, it is considered the first personal computer in history

1969   *United States*: the first connection through Arpanet, the forerunner of the internet, a network including five US universities and research centers

1971   *United States*: Intel starts selling its microprocessors

1975   *United States*: the Altair 8800 hits the market. It is a personal computer to be assembled at home by hobbyists

1977   *United States*: commercial launch of Apple II, the first personal computer intended for a mass market

1982   *World*: 17 million Commodore 64 computers are sold

1983   *United States*: Motorola begins sellling the DynaTAC 8000X, the first portable phone

1984   *United States*: the Apple Macintosh is featured in a television commercial during the Super Bowl. The commercial alludes to George Orwell's novel *Nineteen Eighty-Four*

1985   *United States*: Microsoft releases the first version of Windows

1989   *United States*: Microsoft releases Microsoft Office, which becomes the standard software for intellectual work

1991   *Switzerland*: at CERN in Geneva, Tim Berners-Lee launches the World Wide Web

1995   *United States*: Amazon.com is launched. It claims to be the "Earth's Biggest Bookstore"

1998   *United States*: the Clinton administration approves the Digital Millennium Copyright Act

2000   *United States*: the dot-com bubble bursts, collapsing the NASDAQ index

2001   *United States*: Wikipedia is born. In 2004 it will surpass the one million entries, collected in more than 100 editions in different languages

2004   *United States*: Harvard student Mark Zuckerberg launches thefacebook.com. Facebook quickly expands to become the world's biggest social networking site

2011   *Kazakhstan*: student Alexandra Elbakyan launches Sci-Hub, a website that collects millions of pirated scientific articles. Its goal is "to remove all barriers in the way of science"

2012   *South Korea*: "Gangnam Style," a video by pop star PSY is the first YouTube video to reach one billion views

2013   *United States*: CIA employee Edward Snowden discloses the existence of global secret surveillance programs run by governments in cooperation with telecommunication companies

2017   *China*: the social media and chat app WeChat reaches one billion users

Following this definition, the first computer may be considered the programmable loom invented by Joseph Marie Jacquard in 1801. Still used in the textile industry, albeit in a very different form from the original, the Jacquard loom used a perforated paper roll, similar to those used in automatic pianos which were widespread in the second half of the nineteenth century. The paper contained a set of instructions for the production of textiles with a particular design. By changing the paper roll (the program) you could change the pattern of the product. Inspired by the Jacquard loom, in the mid-nineteenth century the English mathematician Charles Babbage devised two mechanical computers, the difference engine and the analytical engine, both designed to calculate the timetables for the railways that were spreading across England. The problems that Babbage wanted to solve by automating calculation processes were the high cost and low quality of the calculations carried out by hand by human operators. It was the English mathematician Ada Lovelace, who collaborated with Babbage, who first imagined that computers could be programmed. In fact, Lovelace is believed to be the author of the first computer programs in history. While neither machine was built during the life of Babbage and Lovelace, in the twentieth century copies were used to demonstrate their functioning (a working copy can still be found at the Science Museum in London). It is no coincidence that both the Jacquard loom and Babbage's machines were aimed at increasing the efficiency of industrial production and controlling complex organizations such as railways. Indeed, the steps toward the modern computer that were undertaken in the nineteenth century were strongly related to early processes of industrialization and the expansion of the scope and complexity of bureaucracies and administrations (Ceruzzi 2012).

The idea that a new scientific approach could be applied to human affairs, and that social facts were not the effect of the divine will but rather follow specific rules, had been developed in the seventeenth century by the likes of Bacon, Leibniz, and Newton, and was reinforced in the eighteenth century during the Enlightenment. From this new scientific mentality there originated the idea that society could be measured, and social and economic events calculated and to some extent even planned. This way of thinking was greatly reinforced by the development of statistics. Originally called "political arithmetic," statistics responded to nation-states' need to measure and control social events. This was manifested in two major transformations: First, the creation of conscript armies made it essential to know how many soldiers could be provided by a particular city or region, and thus required reliable information on birth rate, mortality, and disease. Second, the new market economy that was expanding during the eighteenth century made more precise economic measurements necessary, as the wealth of a country was beginning to depend on its ability to facilitate and promote trade and manufacturing at a national scale (Mattelart 2003).

In turn, the development of statistics tended to reinforce the idea that the social order was calculable, since it provided data on the basis of which regularities that almost resembled natural laws could be found. In the following centuries statistics generated a strong pressure for the development of new methods of calculation, including new calculating machines. The first computer to be diffused at a national scale was the Hollerith machine, invented at the end of the nineteenth century to solve the problem of the excessive computation time needed to complete the US census – indeed the manual data analysis for the previous census, held in 1880, had required a whole decade. The Hollerith machine processed data in the form of punched cards, a technology derived from the Jacquard loom which remained in vogue until the 1970s. It was based on cardboard cards on which information was recorded by the presence or absence of holes at specific positions. The Herman Hollerith's Tabulating Machine Company distributed punched card computers to governmental agencies and major commercial companies. In 1924, it changed its name to become the International Business Machines Corporation (IBM), and continued to produce computers of this type until the 1970s.

The process of industrialization in the nineteenth century also created demand for new ways of automating the manipulation of information. Production became increasingly automated, and programmable machines such as the Jacquard loom could increase the productivity of industrial workers and standardize their work. The latter aspect was particularly important because skilled workers tended to be politically active, while automation allowed them to be replaced with newly arrived immigrants from the countryside, who had little political experience and were available to work for lower wages. For example, the recruitment of workers from Europe was behind the adoption of semi-automatic assembly lines in Ford factories in the US in the 1920s. But calculating machines were also used to manage the new and complex forms of economic organization that were developed at the turn of the nineteenth and twentieth century. In the United States, emerging corporations started to broaden the reach of their production processes, thus moving from the mere production of goods to the creation of demand by consumers. This gave rise to new disciplines such as marketing, market research, management, and more advanced forms of accounting, therefore increasing the demand for the calculating machines commercialized by the company that was now the market leader: IBM.

World War II provided additional impetus to the development of computers and was a crucial step in shaping computers as we know them today. The war effort required the application of computers for different purposes. For example, there was the need to deal with complex calculations for ballistic purposes and counterintelligence. New theoretical and mathematical approaches to communication were developed around the war, such as Norbert Wiener's cybernetics and Claude Shannon's information theory. By treating communication as the transmission of discrete and calculable units of information, these theories provided some of the basic mathematical tools for the birth of contemporary computing (Gleick 2011). The Manhattan Project, the secret US effort to develop the atomic bomb, gathered hundreds of physicists and engineers and had among its features the need to perform complex calculations. It became one of the hubs for computer innovation during the war years. It was the mathematician and physicist John von Neumann, who had played an important role in the Manhattan Project, who used new theories on information to design the architecture of modern computers. Finally, telecommunications and encryption assumed strategic importance too. Along with hundreds of other British scientists and engineers, the mathematician Alan Turing took part in the effort to decipher the code of Enigma, a machine used by the Germans to encrypt military communications. Turing played a leading role in the construction of Colossus, the first electronic computer built with vacuum tubes. The ability to decrypt German messages gave the Allies a major advantage over the Axis forces. As in other cases in the history of computing, the role of women in this phase has been hidden or minimized. The programmers of ENIAC (Electronic Numerical Integrator and Computer), a vacuum tube supercomputer developed by the United States during the war to process ballistic calculations, were women. Their contract described them as "computers": indeed, programming operations were considered gendered, feminine mechanical tasks of secondary importance compared to designing and building hardware, which was the task of male engineers. With a derogatory term that denied their individual contributions, programmers were informally called "ENIAC girls." Even key characters such as Adele Goldstine, who was in charge of training new programmers and in the 1940s made fundamental contributions to the evolution of modern software, were not recognized by official historiography (Light 1999).

In the postwar years computers began to spread outside of military bases and research centers. The prohibitive cost of computers during the 1950s, their magnitude, and the complexity of the earliest programming languages meant that they remained mysterious devices, managed by a "clergy" of white-coated technicians. The first electronic supercomputer, the IBM Stretch of 1959, sold nine specimens, and the only buyer not directly tied to the military–industrial complex was IBM itself. This puts the alleged prophecy of Thomas Watson, the CEO of IBM until 1956, into context: "I think there is a world market for maybe five computers." At the time a computer could cost tens of millions of dollars, filled an entire room, required enormous amounts of energy, and was incomprehensible for anyone who did not have at least a degree in mathematics. However, the technological innovations of the postwar period quickly changed the performance of computers: during the 1960s IBM, but also the Italian company Olivetti, launched a series of products aimed at medium and large enterprises and public administrations. In 1971 Intel invented the microprocessor, that is, a computer placed on a silicon chip rather than in a room full of electronic tubes. This innovation revolutionized the computer market, dramatically reducing price and size and improving performance. In 1965, one of the co-founders of Intel published what then became known as Moore's law. According to this prophecy, which has since largely been fulfilled, the power of microprocessors would double every 18 months (Moore 1965). Computers spread in organizations and businesses and their impact on the organization of the economy began to grow. Indeed in the late 1970s one could already speak of the emergence of a new society based on computers. Yet if the acceleration described by Moore provided the technological basis for the rise of computers, other factors were crucial in their diffusion as mass products. Already in the 1960s, some of the young engineers and students who were flocking to the new departments of computer science in US universities felt politically close to the counterculture that started dominating American campuses and that would later culminate in the free speech movement and social uprisings of the 1960s and 1970s. These groups would form the first communities of hackers (Levy 2001). Inspired by a democratic ethos, these people saw the hierarchical systems and formal rigor that surrounded computers in large universities and research institutes as a challenge. Conversely, hackers advocated for an active approach to technology and claimed they wanted to modify and use it for new and unforeseen purposes. For example, young students designed the first video games, quite an unpredictable use for computers designed for scientific research or military technology management. In the 1970s this culture merged with the movements of the Californian New Left, which was interested in new information and communication technology and saw computers as instruments of liberation. The *Whole Earth Catalogue*, which was launched by Stewart Brand, was a sort of "instruction manual" for the counterculture. The *Catalogue* also contained computer ads, for example those for building the first "microcomputers" targeted at individual hobbyist, such as the Altair 8800. The counterculture undertook other concrete initiatives to disseminate new technologies. The People's Computer Company was a space that gave public access to new minicomputers to San Francisco residents and radical students at Berkeley. For the first time somebody imagined that computers could become technologies for the development of grassroots communities. Hackers influenced by the New Left imagined they could subvert techno-economic systems through concrete actions of technological manipulation. Their first target was the US telephone network, which in the early 1970s was monopolized by AT&T: hackers found ways to make free phone calls or have open lines they could use to carry out group conversations (a sort of primitive chat room) (Goldstein 2008).

From the relation between hackers and technological counterculture there emerged the first personal computers intended for mass consumption. At the Homebrew Computer Club in Menlo Park, in what would later become Silicon Valley, hackers and hobbyists would exchange ideas, innovations, and hardware components. Among the members of the club were the two founders of Apple, Steve Jobs and Steve Wozniak, and many other future entrepreneurs who became protagonists of the boom of personal computers in the 1980s, as well as famous hackers such as Captain Crunch (Levy 2001). From this and other similar groups there emerged new programming languages such as Bill Gates's Basic (see Section 4.4), as well as devices such as the Apple II. Launched in 1977, the latter was the first computer with a graphical user interface, based on the use of the mouse and directed to the new mass market that was developing in those years. Personal computers were entering the offices of small businesses, professionals, and artisans who could use them to manage their accounting processes. Operating systems such as MacOS (launched in 1984) and Microsoft Windows (which with its 3.0 version launched in 1992 became the market leader), together with software suites such as Microsoft Office, increased the appeal of computers for families. Nevertheless, personal computers initially diffused as platforms for video games, for example with the Commodore Vic20 launched in 1981. The transformation of the computer from a bureaucratic and military technology to a home appliance and entertainment center for families derived from the appropriation and reconfiguration of technologies by actors such as hackers, countercultural activists, Silicon Valley entrepreneurs, and the video game industry. The internet followed a similar path (Rosenzweig 1998).

2.5 The Evolution of Networks

In the 1950s and 1960s people began to think of the computer as a tool not only to perform calculations but also to communicate. Since before the war, the engineer Vannevar Bush, who had played a leading role in US military research and in the Manhattan Project, had imagined the Memex. This imaginary computer was to use a screen to display the texts stored in the machine and create a sort of collective memory mediated by technology. In the early 1960s another researcher linked to the Pentagon, J.C.R. Licklider, theorized the possibility of creating an "Intergalactic computer network" to connect institutions, businesses, and citizens. But the infrastructure that became the ancestor of the internet was in fact Arpanet, a network based on the ideas of Licklider which from 1969 connected supercomputers in US universities and some military centers (Ceruzzi 2012). Arpanet was based on packet-switching technology, which breaks each message into a series of packages that can move through the network independently and are reassembled by the receiver. This architecture is distributed, since there is no central node through which all messages have to pass, and redundant, since information can travel along many different routes (see Section 1.4). The project was launched by the US military research agency ARPA (Advanced Research Program Agency) as part of the technological competition with the Soviet Union after the 1957 launch of the Sputnik, the first artificial satellite, and the discovery of Soviet programs for the realization of a communication network that could withstand a nuclear attack. In fact, in a distributed network the destruction of a single node would not stop the passage of communications, which could take different routes. Soviet leader Khrushchev had also built Akademgorodok in Siberia, an academic city for the study of cybernetics, the science of self-regulating systems that was crucial to the development of information technologies. However, the history of computer networks is the result of the convergence between the military and a number of other actors (Ryan 2010). Although Arpanet was originally designed as a military communication channel to be used to coordinate aeronautical communications, the researchers who worked in major US universities in the 1960s and 1970s profoundly influenced its development as their needs took precedence over military ones. In addition, technical functions such as the email were quickly appropriated and used for the creation of mailing lists for discussing topics that we now associate with digital media but that at the time were completely divergent from official intended uses, such as science fiction or rock music. The TCP/IP protocol that quickly became the standard for digital networks was created to decentralize the control over communications to individual computers or participating nodes and prevent the possibility that someone could control or censor communications. TCP/IP is in fact free, since anyone can use it for free, and open, as it can be implemented on any device and for different purposes. This standard, together with the distributed and redundant structure of Arpanet, is still the basis of the functioning of today's internet.

Arpanet was not alone. Technologies such as BBS (Bulletin Board System), born in the 1970s, were databases of messages and other information contained in personal computers which could be accessed by individual users via the new modem technologies, which allowed computers to transfer information via telephone lines. These communications systems were generated from the bottom and were open to anyone and any topic, from the most serious to the most mundane. In the 1980s, BBSs grew and became genuine alternative networks: it is estimated that in 1991 Fidonet, the largest network of this kind, had come to connect about 10 000 computers. The Well (Whole Earth 'Lectronic Link), created in 1985 by Stewart Brand, the former editor of the *Whole Earth*

Catalogue, used BBS technology to create a "virtual community" (as the phenomenon was baptized by a pioneer of the Well, Howard Rheingold). The Well gathered in one "place" a great amount of information about the alternative cultures of San Francisco (Turner 2006). The network was no longer simply a technology to connect computers, but allowed people to communicate and propagate unorthodox content regardless of state control or censorship. Network technologies developed within governmental initiatives were reappropriated and used for unforeseen purposes too. For example Minitel, the network launched in 1982 by the French postal service, was to be a medium for the exchange of civic information and for online purchases, but was almost immediately dominated by services for the encounter of erotic partners, the famous *messageries roses*. Other state-sponsored initiatives failed, such as the Soviets' plans for a nationwide network (Peters 2016), or were killed for political reasons, such as Chile's Project Cybersyn, which was destroyed after the military coup that toppled the democratic government in 1973 (Medina 2011).

In the 1990s new technological innovations gave birth to the digital networks we know today. In 1991 computer scientist Tim Berners-Lee and other scientists working at CERN in Geneva were working on a communication system for the physicists at the research center. As a result, they wrote and shared the languages and standards that make up the World Wide Web (Ryan 2010). The info.cern.ch site was the first page to be based on Html (Hyper Text Mark-Up Language), a standard used to publish online hypertextual documents in which a section of the text can be marked by tags which describe among other things its function, color, size, and links to which it points. URLs (Uniform Resource Locators) are recognizable addresses that identify content present on a server and allow a computer to request and access it. The URL system makes websites independent from the physical location of their information on a particular computer or server. A webpage can have an Italian URL (.it) but be physically located on a server in Hong Kong. Finally, the HyperText Transfer Protocol (HTTP) is the system upon which online information transmission is based. Berners-Lee and CERN decided to release these innovations without restrictions, so that anyone could use them. This facilitated the spread of a new network of sites linking to each other and which anyone can access, the World Wide Web. In turn, other technologies built upon these standards greatly facilitated the use of computer networks. For example, browsers like Mosaic, which changed its name to Netscape and quickly became the first mass-use browser, provided graphical interfaces that made web surfing easier and faster. The new standards and languages of the World Wide Web and the diffusion of open protocols such as TCP/IP allowed the unification of the various existing networks onto the internet, the network of networks. In 1994,

Berners-Lee launched the World Wide Web Consortium (W3C), the organization that manages the standards for network interoperability. In 1996 the last major actor using alternative and proprietary protocols, Microsoft, adopted TCP/IP for its Windows, completing the unification of the internet.

The spread of networks and the birth of the web were fostered by political choices too. In the course of the 1980s, telephone companies experienced a first wave of liberalization that opened up competition in a traditionally monopolistic market. In 1984, the American giant AT&T was dismantled and the state monopoly British Telecom privatized, creating a new market for telecommunications. In the 1990s, both the United States and Europe launched policies for the construction of technological infrastructures for information and further deregulated the telecommunications market (Harvey 2005). In Brussels in 1995 the richest countries of the world, gathered at the G7 Summit, signed a document which called for the establishment of a global information society, while in 2000 the European Union set the goal of becoming the most dynamic and competitive knowledge economy in the world. Other innovations took place within legal systems. Since 1996, the Digital Millennium Copyright Act (DMCA) has governed intellectual property related to digital media in the United States. The DMCA makes it illegal to subvert or bypass the technologies used for the protection of intellectual property rights such as DRM (Digital Rights Management) technologies that prevent the copying of files or their use outside the countries in which they were purchased. This and other pieces of legislation have reassured the largest producers of content, such as record companies and movie producers, stimulating their interest in the web as a possible business platform.

In the mid-1990s access to the World Wide Web spread rapidly in American and European homes. With access to masses of consumers, the web began to represent an expanding industry. At the time this was primarily based on companies that were then called "dot-coms," such as, for example, commercial portals like Amazon or eBay. It was the so-called new economy: By the end of the decade, any online activity with the ".com" suffix (which stands for commercial) was able to attract disproportionate investments. The companies that were able to portray themselves as geared toward this new open commercial space could raise millions of dollars for business proposals that were often unrealistic and based on inflated expectations. However, this situation gave rise to what in financial terms is called speculative bubble, i.e. a reckless increase in the value of online commerce companies and, in particular, a huge amount of financial investment unrelated to their real value. The bubble burst in March 2000 with the collapse of the NASDAQ index, which represents the trend of technology stocks on the US stock exchange. This resulted in the failure of many dot-com companies, leading to the new technological and economic phase of the 2000s. Successful new corporations were based on interactive web services that fostered direct user intervention in content creation. This new wave of technological and financial innovation was called "Web 2.0," to mark the contrast with the "1.0" e-commerce portals that had been blown away by the bursting of the bubble (O'Reilly 2005). This evolution has not ended, but is an ongoing process that keeps on unfolding in new directions.

2.6   The Future of the Information Society

New information technologies have some fundamental social consequences. In industries, they make possible the automation of production and its reorganization in global networks of factories that can be delocalized in countries with low wages. This tends to reduce both the cost of material production and the bargaining power of the working class. At the same time, the production of intangible goods such as innovation, flexible organization processes and brands becomes more important (see Section 6.4). Conflicts arise between the members of the information society and those who are excluded, as foreseen by Castells, and often their political nature goes unrecognized. Forms of networked social organization affect businesses as well as sociability processes. Furthermore, the global nature of mass culture is reinforced. Political and cultural references may be global and local at the same time, but tend to become less and less linked to national cultures. This seems to at least partly confirm some of the assumptions of the proponents of the idea of an information society, who described the global nature of the new postnational "space of flows" and the pacification of social relations within this space. Yet these utopian hypotheses related to the egalitarian nature of the new information society emerge cyclically and should not be taken at face value. Since the mid-1970s many industrialized countries have witnessed growing income inequalities, with the decline of the industrial working class and its replacement by a new "service proletariat" concentrated in call centers, data entry, sales, and personal services (see Section 6.3). Global inequalities are rising too, with the intensification of the global division of labor between regions that produce raw materials or products, such as some poor African countries, and those who control innovation processes, such as Silicon Valley in California. Services can be outsourced to regions where labor is less expensive and regulated, as in the case of Indian call centers working for global companies (Brophy and de Peuter 2014).

The future of the information society is open and depends on a number of variables. Technological development is only one among many, or rather should be read in the social and economic context in which it occurs. An equally important factor is the evolution of public policies at both the national level and supranational level, for example on telecommunications regulations, workers' rights, or intellectual property. Moreover, the evolution of the information society is related to the actors that guide its development. As we have seen, computers and digital networks are the result of the convergence and overlap of choices made by very different actors: military research, with its demands for centralized communication and computing resources; the scientific community, with its ethos of openness and knowledge sharing; the counterculture and the hacker community, with their ideas about freedom of access and the democratization possibilities offered by distributed networks of computers; corporations, with their marketing and lobbying strategies, as well as their ability to drive innovation or take control of technologies designed for other purposes and transform them into mass commercial goods. In sum, the information society is a project that continues to grow and change, not a historical phenomenon of the past. Today, this project evolves in new directions. For example, the smart city is a project of control of the flows of people, things, and information within the urban context (Vanolo 2014). The platform economy expands corporate control to workers who remain owners of the means of production, for example the car of an Uber driver, but are organized by digital platforms that are able to extract value from their work (Srnicek 2016). Surveillance processes based on an alliance with web corporations allow governments to intercept the digital communications of their citizens for purposes of social control (Lyon 2014). At the heart of all these projects remains the dream of making the world calculable and using this power to organize production and control society. The form taken by digital media, and not just their content, is therefore bound to have an increasing effect on the political and economic life of contemporary societies. In the next four chapters we will analyze these transformations in sociality and identity, forms of cooperation, politics and democracy, and work and economy.

Part II

Transformations

3

Cultures and Identities

Activities mediated by digital technologies such as social media services have an impact on people's life and identity. Digital media foster new forms of interaction and enrich the social life of individuals. Yet the social relations these technologies mediate are not neutral, but rather depend on uneven power dynamics, as well as on cultural and identity factors. Digital media can challenge, but also contribute to cementing such factors.

3.1 Digital Sociality

Social relations have always been influenced by communication technologies. The first political organizations, such as the city-states of antiquity, were born in parallel with writing. Without a means of communication able to cross physical distances and maintain communications over time it would be very difficult to organize a complex social system, collect taxes, and ensure the continuity of the laws or religious customs. The same is true for modern organizations. The invention of printing has changed in depth the forms of production and transmission of culture and knowledge by allowing for social relations to be built across space and time. In the mid-twentieth century, seminal Canadian media theorist Harold Innis studied how modern bureaucratic organizations, such as a state, could not emerge without effective and codified communication systems for the creation and reproduction of documents (1950). Yet media are also essential for creating and maintaining informal groups, as well as for the construction of individual identity. The boom of 1960s youth cultures depended to a significant degree on technologies such as the portable turntable, which allowed people to listen to music outside the home, television, which made possible the almost global and immediate spread of trends and fashions

Introduction to Digital Media, First Edition. Alessandro Delfanti and Adam Arvidsson.

(think of the success of the Beatles), and the phone, which allowed teenagers to interact and communicate with peers. The arrival of digital media and mobile technologies asks for a renewed attention to the relationship between media technologies and social relations as part of the evolution of contemporary information societies.

Digital media have had an unprecedented speed and rate of penetration, as they grew from having a few thousand to several billion users in just two decades. They have also been characterized by the rapid succession of new communication platforms. This differentiation makes it necessary to evaluate different digital technologies in depth, avoiding a simplistic focus on an alleged link between somewhat abstract overall effects of digital technologies and social relations. In the last decades of the twentieth century, two opposing visions seemed to dominate the debate on digital media: on the one hand, they were said to be separated from the social world of everyday "real-life" interactions; on the other, many maintained that they had disruptive effects on all forms of sociality (see Section 3.6). However, today's digital media are characterized by a strong integration between online and offline lives, up to the point that these distinctions seem to lose meaning. In the 1990s, when the internet was accessed via telephone modems, and when the most important platforms were web pages, mailing lists, forums, and Bulletin Board Systems (BBSs), one could reasonably speak of an experience of networks that was distinct from that of the real world: definitions such as "virtual" world or "cyberspace" described a place where it was possible to hide one's real identity by using alternative names or identities. For example, media theorist Lisa Nakamura described "identity tourism" as a fluid process in which internet users use avatars to perform, swap, and even buy identity. Through such processes, Nakamura claimed, "our ideas about race, ethnicity, and identity continue to be shaped and reshaped every time we log on" (2002, p. xi). According to American psychologist Sherry Turkle, in the 1990s users could "experiment with identity by playing out parallel lives" in which they would "shift age, gender, race, and class" (2008, p. 130). Today, social media users tend to post content related to activities, emotions, and events which belong to their daily lives. Mobile technologies such as smartphones and tablets provide access to services like Twitter, Tumblr, or Snapchat anywhere, in a variety of different situations – in the classroom, on the bus, in the office, or at home. Mobile technologies promote an "always on" lifestyle, that is, continuously connected. Therefore, social relationships seem to always be mediated, but that does not make them less significant. Mobile technologies have a crucial role in these processes, as they move the internet into everyday environments – think of carrying a smartphone – thus blending mediated space and material space in the experience of the user (Farman 2012). In this sense the difference between online and offline tends to disappear: online activities, albeit mediated by digital technologies, are fully integrated in everyday social life and social media profiles have a crucial role in people's overall identities. Finally, social media tend to weaken the distinction between public and private, since users share details of their private life publicly via digital platforms. These details become part of individuals' communicative strategies, which thus take place in the context of continuous connection through ubiquitous media (Deuze 2012). This chapter analyzes how digital media, and social media platforms in particular, have become crucial components of social life. Coupled with their technical characteristics, this makes it possible to use them to conduct social research via new methodologies (see Box 3.1). Indeed, in their digital interactions users leave traces of their behavior, interactions, and communications, which can be collected and analyzed for sociological or marketing purposes.

Box 3.1 Digital Methods for Social Research

The progressive expansion of digital and social media has brought to the table interesting consequences for social research. While many studies of the human and social dynamics of digital media are conducted using traditional methods, such as interviews, focus groups, or surveys, a cluster of new research methods based on digital media have been developed over the last few years. These methodologies are collectively referred to as "digital methods" (Rogers 2013) or "computational social science." Indeed social media platforms, as well as e-commerce sites, credit cards, and search engines gather vast amounts of data on user behavior. One could easily say that all our online activities leave traces that lend themselves to be studied by sociologists and other social scientists. With the further expansion of digital media in everyday life that takes place with the use of smartphones and the integration of network technologies in other objects, this ability to collect data will grow further. This is already the case when we use an e-commerce app on our phone or run with a smartwatch that counts the calories we consume.

   Through *big data analytics*, large data sets can be used to extract relevant information and predict trends. From the scientific point of view, digital data are priceless assets. Access to masses of data on entire populations or on nature makes it possible to study phenomena that were previously undetectable. Big data can be used to analyze traffic trends, consumption processes, or patient response to a certain drug. For example, Google Maps provides real-time traffic information by analyzing the position of masses of Android users as they are driving their cars.

Another method based on massive amounts of data is *network analysis*, or the study of networks. This method was born before the rise of digital media, but now uses software to represent media publics, analyze the space they occupy, and study online connections between individuals, for example in order to find out who is most influential on a certain social media. Studying patterns of retweets and likes, network analysts can sort out which Twitter users are able to influence others and generate trends. Instead, *semantic analysis* studies the discourses that develop online. It uses specific software to analyze the occurrences with which, for example, two terms are used in the same communication, and thus aims at extracting hidden meanings. Commercial and political marketing uses these techniques to analyze the content of millions of tweets or comments, and understand whether a certain brand, product, or politician are associated with positive or negative terms. This is called *sentiment analysis*.

Finally, *digital ethnography* follows a different approach, as it aims at understanding in depth the cultures that characterize digital life, with their specific ways of thinking and communicating. This method is an adaptation of traditional ethnographic anthropology to the study of digitally mediated communities or publics, and is based on the observation of forums, social media, mailing lists, or websites, often through the direct participation of the researcher in the life of a community. Studying the cultures and forms of interaction that develop on digital media does not mean focusing exclusively on people. This is an important distinction: in order to study a public of *Game of Thrones* fans, one must take into account the way their interactions are structured by the platform on which they occur (Caliandro and Gandini 2016).

Studying digital platforms presents specific methodological challenges. Currently, much of the data generated by platforms are privately owned. The enormous amount of data collected by Google or Twitter are inaccessible to both public and private researchers, or must be purchased at great cost. In addition, we do not know how social media corporations use them. Large web companies have internal research departments that work on big data analysis in absence of any policy of transparency or public scrutiny. In 2014, US university researchers were criticized for having conducted a psychological experiment in collaboration with Facebook. In it, they studied the emotions of hundreds of thousands of users by secretly manipulating their social media experience (Kramer et al. 2014). Even the study of content that is publicly available, such as comments on a forum or tweets, must respond to the strict ethical standards of social research. Another challenge derives from the opaque features of the algorithms that underpin digital platforms, which are proprietary and not accessible to the researcher. How do we study the functioning of Instagram if we are unable to know how its algorithms select and rank pictures? As noted by scholars grappling with such challenges, critically engaging algorithms requires taking opacity as one of their defining features (Burrell 2016). Hence they must be analyzed as constituted "by institutions, people, intersecting contexts" (Seaver 2017, p. 10). In sum, when facing the inability to open a platform's black box, researchers must use methods such as interviews with programmers or users, and gather information from publicly available documents. This allows the study of algorithms, not in the abstract, but as technical systems with specific effects on specific cultures and communities.

3.2 Social Media

As part of the increased mediatization of everyday social practices and relations, the services that dominate the digital media landscape are social media platforms. Social media are websites based on the ability to build and maintain social ties they provide to users. Many scholars studying social media have proposed that these technologies have assumed a central role in structuring new forms of social relations, and contribute crucially to the construction of personal and group identity (Papacharissi 2010; Couldry and Hepp 2017). While social media are a complex and vast ecosystem populated by dozens of platforms, this section will discuss some common features, such as their ability to code, analyze, and predict social relationships in the service of their business model, as well as their ability to generate and integrate advertising targeting individual platform users.

Early scholarship described social media as web services that allow their users to create a public profile, build a network of contacts whose content and profile information one can see and interact with, and create or join thematic communities or groups (Boyd and Ellison 2007). According to this definition, the first social network was SixDegrees, launched in the US in 1997, although the first service with a mass diffusion was Friendster, which in 2003 had 300 000 users. MySpace was launched in the same year, while the birth of Facebook dates to 2004, although it reached a mass level in 2006. Indeed, during the 2000s, these services experienced a true commercial explosion that placed them among the most important intermediaries between individuals and digital content. In the last decade, social media have proliferated and have occupied an ever-growing position in information societies, both for the massive number of people they reach, and for their continuous and ubiquitous everyday use (Van Dijck 2013b). It is estimated that, in 2018,

Facebook alone, which in recent years has become by far the largest social network, has exceeded two billion active users. Many of these platforms have been developed to facilitate the organization of social relationships around common interests and are at least partly the effect and not just the cause of the emergence of new forms of grassroots sociality (see Section 2.4). This follows a path that has been taken by digital services of the past. For example, the same happened with the first BBS networks, that in the 1980s grew thanks to the groups of users who used them to discuss sex, art, or music. Facebook itself was initially developed to put in touch students at Harvard University, and only at a later stage did it raise the capital that turned it into a commercial enterprise.

There are of course many different platforms, used to organize different social groups, for the most various purposes and in an array of heterogeneous modalities. If some social media are generalist, meaning they are based primarily on the sharing of a variety of content, others are dedicated to specific purposes, media typologies, or demographics. LinkedIn, for example, targets job seekers as well as human resource managers, and is used for professional reasons as a sort of social curriculum vitae. MySpace emerged as a social media service for adolescents but has long been populated almost exclusively by musicians and bands, which use it to target an audience of teenagers. Social media can also be shaped by gender-based differences. For example, Pinterest tends to have a female user base as it facilitates gendered activities, such as craft and fashion. Some exploit geolocalization technologies to locate users' activities and strengthen the relation between physical space and platform interactions. On Foursquare, users receive personalized recommendations of shops to go to near their current location and based on their previous activities or purchases. Grindr is a mobile "hookup" app designed to help gay and bisexual men meet other men in their area. Finally, social networks are not necessarily global, but rather tend to be divided across geographical and linguistic lines. Even if the largest platforms, such as Facebook and Twitter, are used almost everywhere, similar services provided by different actors may be more prevalent in certain geographical areas. This was the case of Orkut, a Google-owned platform that was widely spread in Brazil before being ousted by Facebook. Today, Renren, an Asian platform similar to Facebook, and Sina Weibo, the Chinese equivalent of Twitter, reach hundreds of millions of users. Social media platforms typically integrate services that go beyond the publication of content on their boards or timelines. For example, many of these sites provide chats, instant messaging, email, and telephony, as well as commenting and rating systems.

Social media facilitate and structure social relations and interpersonal communications, as they have the power to shape the type of actions that occur within their services. In fact, the affordances that characterize their technological features offer precise possibilities and at the same time set the limits within which they can be used. As media theorist José van Dijck put it, they do so by "coding relationships between people, things and ideas into algorithms." In turn, "sociality coded by technology renders people's activities formal, manageable, and manipulable, enabling platforms to engineer the sociality in people's everyday routines" (Van Dijck 2013b, p. 12). On social media platforms, all activities generate data which are then analyzed by algorithms and used to shape and organize platform sociality. For example, Facebook is based on the creation of a "social graph," that is, a map of all social interactions among individual users. The generation and analysis of such a map is key for the platform to offer a richer online experience. Facebook uses its data to algorithmically sort out which content is most likely to be interesting for a specific user, and thus generate interactions. This means that it analyzes past interactions in order to predict future behavior (Arvidsson 2016): Facebook estimates how likely it is that a user will interact with another user's post. For example, its algorithms analyze user A's social graph to estimate how likely it is that she will comment on or share a post by user B if that post has already received comments from users C and D. Platforms use this ability in order to foster and increase user participation and sociality, and therefore extract more data (Karppi 2018).

We should note that this feature of social media services is inextricable from their business model: for these platforms, the generation and analysis of data is not a byproduct of online sociality, but rather their primary and most important goal. Their ability not only to mediate sociality but also to "datafy" social interactions is at the core of social media platforms' emergence as key social, political, and economic actors (Couldry and Hepp 2017). Indeed, social media are overwhelmingly owned and managed by private corporations. These companies have developed business models that allow them to extract profits from the information they manage. For the user, most of these services are free, and platforms' revenues do not derive from user fees, but rather from their ability to capture, analyze, and valorize the information users provide to the site. User data is aggregated by software that creates *user profiles* based on their interests and communications, the pages they visit, and their networks of friends (see Chapter 6). The information collected by social media platforms can be sold to third parties, for example marketing agencies, or used directly on the service to provide targeted advertising. Indeed social media platforms thrive on their ability to create advertisements that are compatible with the interests and lifestyles of a user and integrate them as natural components of the communicative environments in which one's relational life develops (Arvidsson 2006). Not all social media are for profit, but non-profit services have struggled to emerge. An example is Diaspora, a Facebook-like service built on free software and on a network of distributed servers. Thanks to its decentralized architecture, no single user or entity can control the system, which depends on many machines on which each user can store their information. Moreover, Diaspora allows for encrypted communications and thus seeks to protect the privacy of its users (Sevignani 2016). This and other similar alternative social media tend to be limited by their inability to reach the critical mass of users which would make them competitive with commercial services.

The rise of social media has effects on many aspects of contemporary information societies. Chapter 5 will discuss how their ability to integrate additional services has made social media key gatekeepers of information, that is, the entry point through which individuals access web content, such as news and other journalistic and political content. Chapter 6 will explore social media's economic power and business models and how they contribute to changing the way we work and consume in more depth. In this chapter we focus on their ever-important role in processes of identity construction.

3.3 Media and Identity

Digital media, and social media platforms in particular, are important instruments through which individuals implement active strategies of identity building. In the mid-twentieth century the sociologist Erving Goffman studied the rituals of self-presentation through which people present themselves in public and construct their identity through communicative practices (1959). This idea has been recalibrated to adapt to digital media and the possibilities offered by social media platforms. Goffman used the theater as a metaphor to describe the way in which people "perform" their identity in public. Following this metaphor, we can argue that social media are one of the "stages" from which individuals represent their own identity through a continuous work of construction. In addition, social media provide individuals with a high control over these processes, therefore allowing for a particularly flexible construction of identity. Opening an account of a particular social media, choosing the photo that characterizes your profile, choosing your friends, joining a particular discussion group, posting politically connoted images or links to music videos are all examples of the ways in which we represent in public some features that we want to be perceived as part of our identity. By revealing something about themselves, for example the way they dress, their hobbies, musical preferences, or political views, individuals perform the continuous work of identity construction discussed by Goffman.

The type of information that we make public may vary within different contexts, i.e. on platforms that are meant to have specific purposes or audiences. For example, professional identity construction is explicit on LinkedIn, while on Facebook the boundary between professional identity and other forms of identity can fade or be difficult to maintain (Van Dijck 2013a). Furthermore, social media are based on the ability to activate and make visible social ties. Therefore the content of the information posted by a user may be less important than the context in which the communication takes place. The photo of a beautiful sunset on a beach posted on the Facebook wall of a friend can be important not only for what it depicts, but especially because it highlights a relationship. In this case it may indicate that the individual who published it was on a vacation with that person. However, social media do not completely determine the identity of a person, but rather contribute to framing it. Many mediated behaviors that have to do with identity performance mirror those that take place offline. For example, researchers have found the prevalence of phenomena of conformism among adolescents who used MySpace in the mid-2000s and strove to be accepted by peers (Boyd 2008).

On today's social media most individuals use their real name. Platform policies had an impact on this change: for example, Facebook prohibits the use of pseudonyms. In other cases, social media do provide a space in which individuals can anonymously express sides of their identity that are deemed socially unacceptable. An example is adolescents using services such as Tumblr or Instagram to spread images and messages favorable to eating disorders, especially anorexia (Boepple and Thompson 2016). This phenomenon, called "thinspiration," has proven resistant to censorship attempts. Indeed teenagers use a myriad of hashtags that change continuously in order to avoid being banned or blocked when other users report a post containing a certain hashtag as improper. The importance of social media for people's identity is also highlighted by phenomena such as the so-called "digital afterlife": it has become common to use a dead person's social media profile, especially on Facebook, to announce their passing and collect messages and memories from friends and relatives. This process can create a kind of "immortality" in which the digital identity of the deceased survives his death (Brubaker et al. 2013). These examples do not mean that there is discontinuity between offline and online identities. Efforts to distinguish them can indeed sound unrealistic. Most relationships mediated by social media are rooted in face-to-face ones. On platforms such as Facebook, people tend to become friends mainly with people with whom they have interactions offline. However, social media are also used to form new relationships, or to enable so-called "latent ties" (Haythornthwaite 2002). An example is friends of friends on Facebook: even if two individuals do not know each other in person, they may realize that they are already part of the same circles and therefore create a connection via the social network. In other cases, such as dating sites or apps, the aim is precisely to build an identity within a space where one can meet new people with whom one hopes to form romantic or sexual relationships. Similar services, such as Badoo, Tinder, or Grindr, have been common for many years. In some countries, such as the United States, couples who have met online represent a significant percentage of new marriages.

Of course, the use of digital media as social spaces is not neutral, but rather influenced by social factors such as age, gender, ethnicity, or class. In response to the spread of connectivity and the integration between the internet and mobile technologies in the 2000s, media scholars even discussed the rise of a new generational subject. The definition "digital natives" (Prensky 2001) was meant to describe young people born in close contact with computers and the internet through mobile phones, tablets, and video games consoles. The formula was used to distinguish them from "digital immigrants," that is from people who were born before the advent of the internet and came of age in a world dominated by print and television. Furthermore, the natives would also be bearers of new forms of sociability and identity strongly marked by the characteristics of these technologies. The concept resonates with common sense ideas of how so-called "millennials" interact with digital media. However, the concept of "digital natives" has been largely abandoned, since it tends to hide the differences in *how* people use the internet and social media, even among those who are born into a world dominated by these technologies. Furthermore, it focuses narrowly on generational differences while ignoring those based on social class, gender, and ethnicity.

Indeed digital technologies are far from being "blind" to gender or race, and can reproduce gender- or race-based rather than generational divisions. First, different services can be populated by different demographics or respond to specific gender-based logics. For example, 4chan, a famous anonymous forum where many memes that subsequently spread on social media are created, has a strong masculine component. In this context, the local subculture makes use of sexist and homophobic insults that are met with opposition only from a minority of users (Milner 2013). Parental online forums used to discuss issues such as nursing or vaccines can be gendered in an opposite way, as male individuals tend to assume a subaltern role – for example, they may introduce themselves as another user's husband. Furthermore, research on internet cultures has indeed shown how digital media tend to represent both gender (Gill 2007) and race (Nakamura 2008) according to stereotypes, thus contributing to reinforcing them. Recent feminist scholarship has highlighted several facets of such phenomena and how they intersect with the functioning of social media platforms. For example, a platform such as YouTube relies on human moderators, often working in developing countries, to filter and remove violent, racist, or homophobic content after it has been flagged by users. These workers act as gatekeepers for the platform and have to abide by its commercial motives. Indeed, upsetting videos with racist content may collect millions of views on YouTube, and are therefore used to show commercials. In sum, social media platforms decide on removing content depending not only on the likelihood of it causing offense, but also on its commercial value. Content moderators are exposed to this disturbing material while lacking the power to decide based on their sensibility and politics (Roberts 2016).

The representation of identities is not the only lens through which to look at gender and race in digital media, and intersects with other dynamics. Feminist theorists of technology have long argued that studying design is key to understanding gender relations in contemporary societies (Wajcman 2000). Following this call, scholarship on digital media has started focusing on how cultural and political values are not simply represented, but rather inscribed in or reproduced by "the machine." Black feminists such as Safiya Noble have called for a politically infused analysis of the "algorithms of oppression" that reinforce inequalities while presenting themselves as neutral. In her research, Noble has shown how the algorithms that underpin Google Search reinforce stereotypes. For example, terms like "hot" or "sugary" tend to be the primary representations of black girls on Google searches (2018). There are many other instances of algorithms that reinforce inequalities. For example, companies producing face recognition software have been criticized for producing technologies which work better with light skin. This is part of a legacy of racism in image technologies. In the 1950s and 1960s the so-called "Shirley" cards used by photographers to calibrate their equipment were only based on white women, thus normalizing whiteness (Roth 2009). In order to be properly captured by the film used for movies in the 1970s and 1980s, black actors had to use specific make up.

The algorithms that underpin the functioning of digital media produce what scholars have called "algorithmic identity" not directly related to our racial or gender identity but rather inferred based on algorithmic evaluations of our online behavior. This has to do with economic rationales. Indeed, algorithms used to profile users "calculate" gender and race, so to speak, by producing statistical models used for marketing or other purposes. In these processes, gender and race become marketing categories rather than negotiations about gender roles or socially constructed racial groups (Cheney-Lippold 2017). Therefore, a user who visits a website that is classified as "manly" would be considered by marketing algorithms as more likely to be male, and thus move from 73% man to 85% man, regardless of how female they may consider themselves. Facebook does not ask users their race or sexual orientation but, depending on what they do on the platform, it may assign them something it calls "ethnic affinity." If you live in Texas and occasionally write messages in Spanish, it might assign you to the "Hispanic" category. Interestingly, Facebook has "ethnic affinity" categories for African Americans, Asian Americans, and Hispanics among others, but none for Caucasians. Regardless of behavior, social relations, and geographical location, Facebook won't put them in the "white" category, because that category does not exist. Scholars studying such phenomena have come up with definitions such as "platformed racism" to describe how seemingly technical decisions amplify racist discourses and reproduce social inequalities (Matamoros-Fernandez 2017). Indeed these calculations have material effects, as the identities assigned by algorithms are used to predict consumer behavior and select which content will be shown to a certain user. Facebook's choices reinforce the idea that white is "normal" and shapes its ads accordingly. On some job-seeking platforms, users who are considered women are less likely than men to be shown job ads for managerial positions.

Box 3.2 The Gender of Artificial Intelligence

Studying artificial intelligence (AI) can help us understand how gender stereotypes are built into digital technologies. The diffusion of AI technology in consumer products has made the interaction with artificial humans commonplace. AI is used to provide services that mimic human interactions, such as chatbots, personal assistants, or robots. In the male-dominated world of technology, AI tends to be designed by male engineers, but also imagined and represented in fiction by male movie writers and producers. This is reflected in how gender is built into AI. For example, most personal assistants have female voices: think of Apple's Siri, Microsoft's Cortana, or Amazon's Alexa, although other companies have used male voices, for example, for Google Now. Among other characteristics, these AI assistants tend to be submissive, a personality trait associated with femininity. Indeed, the tasks they perform are gendered, as care and housework tend to be associated with women. This is part of a longer story of gendered technologies. One of the first chatbots was Eliza, a program created in the 1960s at MIT to mimic a psychotherapist. You can still find and chat with her online. By contrast, most AI-based robots in science fiction are male: think of R2-D2 and C-3PO in *Star Wars*, or HAL 9000 in Stanley Kubrick's *2001: A Space Odyssey*. These robots tend to be proactive and powerful. Finally, gender-neutral AI is not uncommon in personal assistants, but rare in sci-fi robots. In sum, AI can reproduce and reinforce existing gender-based stereotypes.

Finally, some of the most important differences in the use of digital media result from different levels of access to what sociologists call "cultural capital." Individuals with a high level of education who are used to searching and using information in a thoughtful and creative way tend to exhibit these characteristics in all spheres of life, including those mediated by digital technologies. On the contrary, people who are accustomed to a more passive use of information tend to be less critical and less reflective in the use of digital media too. People who have a life full of activities and social relations, perhaps because they are members of associations, volunteer for a non-profit, or are politically active, tend to make a richer and more varied use of digital media compared to those characterized by a lower richness of social relations. In sum, differences in social class, gender, cultural traditions, or geographical area may be more important than age in influencing the different ways in which people use digital media (Van Dijck and Hacker 2011). For example, online services used by diasporic communities that are united by the experience of migration are used to maintain and strengthen ties based on ethnicity and nationality. At the same time, individuals belonging to different social classes can use digital services and technologies in completely different ways even within the same territory. In order to capture the flexible nature of online identities, media studies have focused on how they are organized as publics of media content.

3.4   Communities or Publics?

Often times, groups of people formed via digital media, such as fans discussing a movie franchise on Reddit or individuals creating and sharing memes in a forum, are described as communities. Yet the social sciences use this word to address very specific social phenomena. For sociologists, the term "community" implies a strong relational density: the members of a community interact with each other and share meanings, practices, values, and binding norms. Therefore, not all relations built through digital media should be described as communities. Classic sociological theory distinguishes between two forms of social relations. On the one hand there are community relations, characterized by high levels of trust and mutual understanding. These relationships are articulated in tight-knit forms: for example, in a small rural town everyone knows everyone and traditional informal rules apply. In a community the group has priority over individuals, and the rules governing social life are bounding and at times oppressive. On the other hand, modern social relations are characterized by the importance of associations that abide by formal and explicit rules, such as bureaucratic organizations, political parties, trade unions, or professional associations. Rights and obligations are governed by laws, and the relation between individual autonomy and social norms is more balanced. In the latter case, the sense of identification with the community is less intense, forms of interaction "colder" but also less oppressive (Tönnies 1912). In turn, levels of loneliness are potentially higher. Associational societies make individuals more free but also lonelier than communities.

The spread of social media has been interpreted as the emergence of a third form of social relations, which has been described with definitions such as *networked individualism* (Rainie and Wellman 2012). Networked individualism is the result of the coordination of the large amount of opportunities and individual choices enabled by digital media. Individuals tend to belong to a multitude of different social networks, often disconnected from each other. In each network, individuals can show or develop a particular aspect of their identity. There are no hegemonic characteristics, given that people have the opportunity to make a set of plural choices that shape their overall identity. The concept of networked individualism is at least partially indebted to Georg Simmel's theory of modern life, a founding sociological work (1908). Studying the social relations that developed in large cities in the early twentieth century, Simmel showed that the typical individual experience of modernity is characterized by the simultaneous belonging to different "circles." People construct their identity by belonging to groups that are very different from each other, and therefore are characterized by distinct codes of conduct and norms: for example, an individual may belong to a political party, a hockey team, and a neighborhood library's book club.

While these theories were developed in the early twentieth century, they are useful in understanding how an active construction of an array of social circles has been greatly facilitated by the spread of digital media. Social media make it much easier to identify and contact people with whom an individual may share passions, interests, and values. These interactions can take place on different platforms: a Twitter hashtag, an online forum, the comments section of a blog, an online video game, or an internal discussion list used by Wikipedia editors. Whether it is parents who discuss childcare products, patients who talk about their disease and exchange advice on treatments and doctors, fans of a pop band, people who share the same political views, or macrobiotic enthusiasts, digital media facilitate the proliferation of groups organized around common interests or lifestyles. This phenomenon has been described through definitions such as *networked collectivism* in which groups of people held together by weak bonds, such as the interest in childcare products, can build and maintain lasting and effective networks (Baym 2007). To emphasize the difference with groups that share stronger bonds, such as family members, other authors have described these new forms of sociability based on digital media as *networked publics* rather than communities (Boyd 2010). Castells (2009) has called these forms of interaction "mass self-communication": each individual can communicate with the audiences that surround them, contributing to the emergence of shared opinions and information (see Chapter 4).

These forms of interaction organized around media content can be transient and ephemeral, tend not to be lasting, and often take place among strangers (Warner 2002). This of course does not exclude that within these publics smaller communities with deeper levels of interpersonal interaction may appear. Yet the term "public" indicates that these collectives are less dense and all-encompassing than communities. Being part of a public of parents on a forum is not necessarily a binding element for the identity of a person, as opposed to being a member of a local religious community. But at the same time, networked publics are denser than mere networks. A "network" is simply a technical term for a set of links. But the public constituting a forum for amateur ufologists is something more than a network, since it is equipped with common passions and values that represent a motivation for the participants – "we must find out the truth about aliens." A public can be characterized by a shared social imaginary, which also implies ethical and political choices – "we must find out the truth about aliens, because this information should not be limited to the government, which tries to keep it secret." A public formed around a political event may create affective bonds rather than merely sharing attention to media content. In her analysis of political mobilizations mediated by social networking services, communication studies scholar Zizi Papacharissi defined such interpersonal bonds as "structures of feelings" created by storytelling. According to her, "technologies network us, but it is our stories that connect us" (2016). Therefore publics, although less dense and less binding than communities for the construction of one's personal identity, offer their members the opportunity to identify with a common cause and obtain from other members a recognition of their contribution to this common cause. The publics of digital media can be social entities with a particular vision of the world.

Finally, communities tend to last over time and retain the same members. Getting out of a community can be difficult, precisely because of the profound links upon which it is based. On the contrary, networked publics can be much more fluid and transient. An extreme example would be a public formed around a hashtag on Twitter. The hashtag can create an interest and intense involvement tied to a particular event, for example the concert of a foreign rock star in Sweden, which lasts for a few days or even a few hours and then evaporates. Even in the most enduring publics, such as the guilds of the online role-playing game *World of Warcraft*, turnover is very high: it was estimated that these groups may lose up to 25% of their members every month (Duchenaut et al. 2006). In sum, publics can be much more transient social phenomena than communities. In premodern communities, identity was dictated by tradition. In modern associational societies, identity depended in part on individual choices, such as the decision to join a particular association, group, or party, but from those choices derived binding rules of conduct. In networked publics, identity is built through a series of choices. Individuals choose the publics to which they belong, the degree of involvement, and how much importance each of these publics has for their identity. An individual can belong to a public that shares the passion for of a particular sexual practice, but that can be of little importance for their overall identity, or even remain secret. The opposite is possible too, as other individuals can decide to build most of their identity around the involvement in a public; for example, people who participate in queer or asexual publics in order to reiterate the importance for their identity of sexual choices that do not comply with heterosexual and homosexual canons. Social media platforms such as Tumblr allow for such groups not only to form in opposition to dominant cultures, but also to reach an appropriate audience (Renninger 2015). Yet the weak and transient nature of the bonds that generate a public means that they are not necessarily decisive for one's life. With some obvious exceptions, such as belonging to groups of religious or political extremists, one can typically belong to many publics even if they are very different from each other. Identity can be seen as the overall result of these memberships.

Box 3.3 Sexuality and Pornography

"Sex" is one of the most clicked on and searched for terms on the internet. Since the time of the internet's ancestors, such as BBSs or the French Minitel, sex has been a crucial engine of growth for digital media, both for its ability to attract users, and because it has stimulated new and unexpected forms of use that had a role in technological evolution. The online sex market in the US alone is estimated to be worth around 100 billion dollars a year, although in recent years the industry has reported declines in profits due to piracy and new distribution models of pornographic content. This wealth is reflected in investments: for example, porn production companies have contributed to the development of new streaming video technology, online ads, and even 3D immersive technologies. Indeed, corporate websites such as PornHub represent a significant percentage of internet traffic, and may receive more visits than services such as Netflix or Amazon. As in similar industries, this field has witnessed a partial dissolution of the borders between consumer and producer: people can easily create erotic or pornographic content and distribute it via online platforms. Although they are not limited to online services, these new forms of production and distribution of pornography have given queer, gay, or feminist publics new spaces in which to actively produce pornographic content. This contributes to changing the aesthetic conventions of porn, which had historically been directed to an audience of white heterosexual men. For example, many have argued that queer porn can be a "generative space" in which specific desires, identities, and politics can become visible, be negotiated, and evolve (Smith et al. 2015). In sum, by giving voice to a more diverse set of sexual subcultures, digital media are not only crucial distribution infrastructures, but also help redefine forms of sexual expression.

3.5 Reputation and Influence

The emergence of networked publics and the importance of digital media as tools for building social relations are intimately linked to changes in the way personal reputation is formed. In a sense, digital media materialize ideas that have been present along the history of the information society, as they further the idea that social facts can be the subject of rational calculations. Reputation is a judgment on a person which is expressed on the basis of public information. It is not essential to know a person to have an opinion. All the citizens of ancient Rome recognized Cicero's reputation, even those who had never met him in person. Furthermore, citizens directly contributed to determining his reputation, talking badly or well of him, and therefore generating buzz and opinions on the basis of the information they had access to. The same happens in the celebrity world: only a few individuals know Kim Kardashian in person, but millions know her reputation and make judgments about her. Digital media amplify and transform the way in which reputation is created and fed, and provide people with new tools to manage it. The importance of digitally mediated forms of reputation in contemporary societies has been captured by definitions such as "reputation economy" (Gandini 2016).

Members of a public acquire reputation according to the way other members judge their contributions, for instance the relevance of a piece of content contributed to a blog, or its adherence to the specific ethical codes of the public. The reputation of the programmers who participate in a free software project depends not only on their technical skills, but also on their ethical and political commitment: for example, the energy and time they invest in resolving conflicts or helping new members, or how much they respect the expectations of the community by avoiding any interaction with Microsoft or Apple, which are considered antithetical to the values of free software (Coleman 2005). Many services and platforms provide software systems that calculate and communicate the reputation of their members, which in turn determines their status. These systems are based on forms of rating: users can evaluate other users by assigning a score that describes their adherence to the social norms that allow the proper functioning of the platform. The software aggregates these scores, adding them up or using more complex calculations, and uses them to generate a rating, often expressed as a number or represented with a symbol. Reputation ensures a better position within the group, or better chances of success for a worker (see Section 6.3). For example, members with a higher reputation on the auction website eBay conclude transactions more easily, as other buyers or sellers tend to trust people who, according to eBay's rating system, have always paid for their purchases on time or have always sold objects in mint condition. Reputation is even more important for non-profit services like Couchsurfing, a website for the encounter between the demand for and offer of hospitality for travelers who want to crash on the couch or in the guest room of other members. Hosting or being hosted by a stranger is an action that can be dense with risks and expectations and implies no monetary rewards. Therefore, those who offer their home to strangers may decide to accommodate only users with a high rating, while travelers looking for hospitality in a new city can select the homes that have accumulated positive comments. Whenever someone is hosted, the rating system is upgraded. Indeed, both the host and the guest comment and vote on their experience (Lauterbach et al. 2009). While ratings are crucial, other factors play a role in determining how trust and reputation are built in such platforms. For example, a study of Airbnb users demonstrated the importance of profile photographs in the determination of prices on the platform: customers whose profile pictures were perceived as being more "trustworthy" tended to be favored over others (Ert et al. 2016). Other studies demonstrate the persistence of discrimination. For example, an experiment conducted on Airbnb in the United States showed how users with distinctively African American names were less likely to be accepted than users with white-sounding names (Edelman et al. 2017).

While skewed by persistent biases and prejudices, reputation may determine the ability of an individual to interact with a public in a productive way. Yet it also affects the enjoyment and satisfaction that can be derived from the interaction with a specific public. Participating in a *Star Trek* fan-weekend will be much more fun if you have a good reputation in the public of fans than if you are a complete stranger. Reputation tends to determine the intensity of the interactions an individual can establish with a particular public, and therefore the importance of that public for her overall identity. If you spend a lot of time and energy to build a good reputation in a particular public, it is likely that the interactions within that public are important to the construction of your personal identity. As discussed in Section 3.4, the communicative nature of networked publics and the structure of social media platforms mean that identity cannot be simply lived but must also be communicated and performed. Individuals create a communicable version of their identities – some call this "personal brand" – which may include certain aspects of their lives while hiding others (Hearn 2008). Performing identity therefore becomes a rational and reflective process aimed at being communicated, in particular on social media.

The construction of a personal brand takes place in a particular media environment, in which the technological characteristics of the platform influence and structure the labor of self-branding. Danah Boyd has proposed that social media communications are persistent, replicable, scalable, and searchable (2010). These features have precise implications. The persistence of objects communicated on digital media makes them survive over time. Therefore, past events or choices can have an ongoing impact on one's identity. Some platforms, such as Facebook, make our past visible and act as a sort of "biographical archive." Replicability of content means that the communications that occurred in a particular environment can travel across different media or be combined with communications that occurred in another environment, creating something new. A photo posted on Instagram can be sent to a WhatsApp group or tweeted, thus leaving the context for which it had been created. Scalability means that content can spread very quickly and reach much bigger publics than those for which it was initially intended. This can be a resource for those seeking attention. But this phenomenon can also apply to content that users do not necessarily want to spread outside of limited circles. For example, the boundaries between communications with friends and with coworkers can be easily crossed. Finally, digital content is easily searchable, and thus easy to find. Hiding unwanted information can be difficult, while search engines can help find information on a person. For example, individuals who intend to begin a romantic or professional relationship with somebody can find information about them that was destined to remain in a private or different context. By analyzing their social media profiles, an employer may find out the political orientation of a prospective worker.

The evolution of social media has also generated the emergence of services that attempt to measure and quantify the influence of individuals. Services like Klout or Kred measure the influence of the communications that take place around a user, providing a numerical estimate of the impact of their communication activities on the behavior of other individuals. The algorithms that underlie these systems calculate the size of the network reached by an individual and their ability to generate interactions. For example, Klout calculates the number of people reached by content posted on social media such as Facebook and Twitter and interactions generated in the form of replies, shares, likes, or comments. Social media for academics and researchers such as Academia.edu allow users to upload research papers and then use data on downloads, ratings, and social interactions to calculate their impact on the community at large (Duffy and Pooley 2017). In addition, these systems take into account the influence of the people who interact with a certain user: if a message on Twitter or a paper on Academia.edu is reposted by a user who the system deems to be highly influential, this interaction is assigned a higher score than one with someone that has a limited influence. The relevance of these systems is questionable. On the one hand, the algorithms on which they are based are accused of being poor and not truly reliable. On the other, their attempt to evaluate the communicative interactions on the basis of quantitative parameters does not take into account the many other aspects of human communication. However, these systems have in some cases a real impact on individuals. In some professional fields, for example, rankings that calculate one's influence can be decisive for employment opportunities. Fashion bloggers who are able to mobilize large numbers of other users thanks to the size and strength of their network of contacts, as well as their social and communicative skills, can be hired by marketers or clothing companies. Indeed these types of user are considered crucial resources for the success of a marketing or political campaign. In areas such as design or media production, the digitally mediated reputation and personal brand of freelance workers are important factors that determine their ability to access the labor market (Gregg 2011). In all the above examples, the public and private identity of a professional may overlap. Indeed social media activities tend to be based on the sharing of aspects of one's private life even when meant as interactions with broader or different publics.

3.6 Critiques of Digital Sociality

Forms of sociality mediated by digital technologies have been faced with many critiques. Among the most common points of contention is the claim that networked relationships tend to be colder and less engaging than face-to-face interactions. For some, the result of an increasingly mediated world would be a set of individuals who are emotionally disconnected from each other, and thus united by weak bonds and super-ficial forms of solidarity that are likely to fall apart when facing chal-lenges. This criticism is partly founded. Compared with traditional communities, the ties that characterize contemporary online publics are less strong and generate less stringent forms of solidarity. However, not having strong social ties with the people with whom one shares some interests or discussions does not prevent them from satisfying their need for affectivity in different spaces or with different people. Moreover, the weight of different forms of sociality depends on individuals, who may choose to be more or less bound to a certain public.

Other critics of digital sociality argue that the immersive experience provided by digital media tends to absorb people into a parallel world, and therefore isolate them. This idea was already present in science fiction written at the dawn of digital networks. In the cyberpunk world described in the 1980s by US novelist William Gibson, people immersed themselves in a virtual world, a cyberspace directly connected to their cerebral cortex in which they lived a parallel life without having to interact with other human beings. According to Turkle (2011), the spread of the internet, and particularly of ubiquitous social media accessible via mobile technologies, creates a situation in which individuals no longer interact with their neighbors but are rather absorbed in a parallel world made of Snapchat messages and Instagram posts. According to this view, social media would project us in a world in which we are "alone together." Turkle includes in this framework many technologies, such as robots used to foster social interactions in patients suffering from senile demen-tia. Human interactions would become scarce and replaced by interac-tions with machines that try to simulate, with varying degrees of success, the warmth and authenticity of human affectivity. The picture painted by Turkle is recognizable in situations like a subway car in which individuals sitting side by side are immersed in their smartphones, or a classroom where students interact on Facebook or Instagram instead of listening to the lecture. They are physically present together, but mentally absorbed in their private worlds. Alone together, indeed. This and other similar views are part of a long narrative about the loss of sense of community and "warm" social relations that, since the late nineteenth century, accompanies modernization processes and the emergence of new com-munication technologies. The Israeli sociologist Eva Illouz called the emergence of such forms of sociality "cold intimacies" (2007). However, empirical studies carried out since the 1990s seem to provide a very dif-ferent picture. Users of digital media tend to have larger and more diverse social networks than those who do not use them. Internet users are not inherently less prone to visit their neighbors and tend to have a richer community life than people who do not use digital media. Digital media do not keep people away from the public space, but rather can be considered a factor that nurtures their rich social life (Rainie and Wellman 2012). Social media are an integral part of our social life, and are not a means to leave it. They do not impoverish social relationships. Rather, the way in which people interact with each other can change with the use of these technologies.

When analyzing such critiques we should keep in mind that new communication technologies always tend to generate waves of criticism and even moral panic (Cohen 1972). These forms of so-called techno-pessimism are nothing new: fears linked to the social role of digital technologies are part of a much longer history of mistrust toward new media. In eighteenth-century Europe the novel was accused of diverting young women from their social roles and immersing them in an unreal world of dreams. In the 1930s some argued that movie theaters and jazz music diffused via radio would destroy the moral fiber of younger generations. In the 1960s television was accused of destroying communities and traditional cultures; in the 1980s videotapes were blamed for generating violence in youth; this accusation was then turned against video games in the 1990s. In recent years sexting, that is, the exchange of explicit sexual messages, pictures, or other types of content via mobile phones, has created diffused anxieties related to services such as Snapchat. The latter is an app-based service to exchange via smartphones photographs or videos that do not get stored in the phone's memory but rather "disappear" after a few seconds. The use of such services by adolescents has raised fears based on gender stereotypes. In the public discourse, girls are portrayed as too uninhibited or victimized, even if their sexting activities are consensual. Furthermore, girls tend to be seen as less in control of technology and more passive or clueless than boys. The novelty of the technology makes it more common to witness fears focused on a limited number of isolated cases of sexual abuse that happen within millions of perfectly acceptable interactions (Hasinoff 2012). For example, landline phones are regularly used by sexual predators, but nobody would blame the technology itself, which has long been accepted and is now seen as neutral.

Privacy is another area of emerging concern. Indeed, the proliferation and extension of the mediated environments that organize our social and individual lives has important effects on privacy. Social media platforms have undermined old concepts of privacy as based on the ability to live a private life not visible in public. In a sense this idea of privacy had already been undermined with the advent of television and the subsequent exposure of the private lives of celebrities and politicians. Yet social media push all individuals to share, in public, personal and intimate details of their private lives, from holiday photos on Instagram to the results of medical tests on patient forums. Google's CEO, Eric Schmidt, once argued that "if you have something that you don't want anyone to know, maybe you shouldn't be doing it in the first place" (cited in Smith 2010), reiterating that individuals are to be considered responsible for their own privacy. Yet it would be difficult to ignore the need for stringent rules that protect privacy or for technologies that allow the removal of unwanted information from the public view. Furthermore, issues around individual privacy intersect with the pervasive forms of surveillance and social control that both governments and corporations put in place through digital media (see Section 5.5). Clashes regarding access to information held by internet services by, for example, the police, or the use of personal social media data for marketing purposes emerge cyclically. And yet several studies show that the explosive growth of social media goes hand in hand with a change in the perception of these problems. The idea of having two completely separate spheres, i.e. a public and a private life, cannot be considered an accurate description of digitally mediated sociality. On the one hand, individuals have partially given up a conception of privacy as a right to a non-accessible private sphere. Indeed such an arrangement would undermine one's chances to fully participate in digital sociality. On the other hand, people tend to actively negotiate privacy by controlling available information about them or the social interactions they have in different mediated spaces. Individuals are able to choose what kinds of communication relating to their private life they carry on through which media. Also they know the cultural and informal communication codes that characterize different platforms and contexts. For example, although they are seen as being exposed to the dangers represented by sexual predators, teenage social media users have been shown to be able to exercise control over their online life and negotiate with peers methods to avoid unwanted interactions (Marwick and Boyd 2014). A critical approach to social media remains necessary if we are to find solutions to grant digital media users the right to privacy as well as access to mediated spaces.

4

From Collaboration to Value

Digital technologies facilitate the active participation of individuals in media production, and underpin processes of collaboration among peers. The content generated by internet users is critical to the success of web corporations and has transformed traditional mass media. Free software, open source applications, and Wikipedia are examples of digital collaboration that rely on a culture of participation. Yet the value created through collaborative processes is often appropriated by digital corporations.

4.1 Collaborative Media

Among the technological, economic, and organizational transformations of information societies, an important place is occupied by the increased user participation and active collaboration in content production. This evolution is part of the trend toward broadening access to information and using it to democratize productive and political processes, a core element of the information society project. In its most recent incarnations, such expansion has repercussions on all areas of cultural production and beyond, from journalism to science, from software production to marketing. Most digital services are in fact interactive and allow for public participation, or even rely fully on forms of production completely entrusted to users. Digital platforms offer possibilities for users to become content producers, or contribute to assessing and improving the content provided by a service. Wikipedia is written and edited by its users; Instagram would not exist without the content produced and posted by its public; hotels are ranked on TripAdvisor thanks to an aggregation of their clients' reviews. Tools such as social media, blogs, video streaming services, wikis, tagging systems, and resources for information sharing represent the technical basis of this transformation

Introduction to Digital Media, First Edition. Alessandro Delfanti and Adam Arvidsson.
© 2019 John Wiley & Sons, Inc. Published 2019 by John Wiley & Sons, Inc.

which, however, relies on a set of legal and cultural changes too (Benkler 2006). Legal systems have adapted copyright laws to facilitate the spread of self-publishing platforms such as YouTube. At the same time, collaboration on such platforms would not be possible without the spread of a culture of participation that has become an integral part of processes of information and knowledge production.

One of the most common definitions of the outcome of these processes is *user-generated content*. According to theorists like Henry Jenkins (2006), a culture of participation via digital media is based on the removal of barriers to the expression of creativity, on willingness to share content, and on the feeling that one's contribution is valuable to a community. This is not fully new, as media participation preceded digital media. For example, forms of public participation in media production have been at the center of alternative media such as community radio stations or independent newspapers for decades, as these alternative media saw public participation as a chance to establish democratic forms of communication and exit the sphere of commercial mass media. However, technological and economic changes related to digital media have furthered these forms of interaction with the media industry. In fact the phenomenon has exploded since the 2000s, with the transition from static forms of one-way digital communication to more collaborative web services, which deeply changed the media and cultural industry (Harrison and Barthel 2009). The content of broadcast media such as television and press is directed from a central hub that produces and sends the message to many peripheral receivers. The audience of broadcast media can choose what content to read or watch, but cannot contribute personally or provide direct feedback to content producers. In the early years of the emergence of the commercial internet many online services had similar features. They widened the range of choices available to the public, but did not provide new possibilities to become an active part of communication processes. Today, however, digital applications and services enable a higher level of interaction between users and the service itself. The user assumes a central role, as everyone has the opportunity not only to enjoy content, but to create and edit it too.

Examples of collaborative applications are many and very different, but all emphasize participation, content creation, and information sharing. Blogs are online diaries or journals, which compose what has been called the *blogosphere*, that is, an environment made up of blogs in communication with each other. This is strongly intertwined with social media, rating systems, and microblogging platforms such as Twitter. Thanks to blogging platforms such as WordPress, producing a blog does not require specific technical skills. Therefore, writing for a public is no longer reserved to journalists and other professional writers. Wikis are collective writing softwares, which allow multiple users to simultaneously work on the same text or document: the best known example of a wiki-based service is Wikipedia, the non-profit online encyclopedia written collaboratively by thousands of users around the world. Commercial services like YouTube or Instagram allow users to publish, tag, and share videos and photos, respectively. The success of these services is due not only to the use of software for online publishing, but also to the spread of low-cost equipment such as cameras, as well as software for video or photo editing, which can be installed on most personal computers and phones. Online marketplaces and stores, such as eBay or Amazon, use the information produced by their users to improve their service. On Amazon, customers write reviews or rate commodities, thus providing valuable information which the platform aggregates and uses to present its products to other clients.

Mashup services are not too different, as they facilitate the aggregation of information from different sources to create a site or application. A popular example is Google Maps, an interactive map service to which users can add information, thus creating customized maps that aggregate information from users and other websites. Another mashup platform that takes advantage of the possibilities opened up by the spread of smartphones is Ushahidi, a non-profit service that creates interactive maps by aggregating information sent via email and SMS. Ushahidi has played a crucial role in events in which traditional media were blocked or rendered inoperable by natural events, as in the case of the political turmoil after the 2007 elections in Kenya or the earthquake in Haiti in 2010. In both cases, Ushahidi used the information and evidence provided by its users to create maps that anyone could consult and contribute to, making them evolve in real time (Okolloh 2009). Through tagging technologies users can associate content with a label that allows other users (or software) to understand what type of content it is, to what it is connected, and so on. Rating systems permit individuals to vote on, or rather provide a numerical rating to, a certain piece of content. This is how Amazon works, but many other platforms for reviews have integrated rating systems. Think of how ratings are produced for restaurants on Yelp, or for university teachers on RateMyProfessors.com. Rating systems work when many individuals assess something, and therefore the overall "grade" attributed, for example, to a restaurant on Yelp is an aggregate result rather than a single review. The participation of many users makes rating systems more reliable and limits the effect of incorrect or biased reviews.

The emergence of collaborative media is not just a matter of technology. Together with the birth of collaborative software and platforms we have witnessed the emergence of a culture of participation that leads consumers to contribute more directly to information production, breaking out from the canonical dynamics of the cultural industry. Fan communities have historically been the object of important studies of this changing media system based on *participatory cultures* (Jenkins 2006). Fans (of a band, a movie, a television series) are increasingly actively involved in the production of alternative content, for example in the forms of videos, fiction, video games, or cartoons. One of the cases taken as an example by Jenkins was the community of *Star Wars* fans. But thanks to the widespread availability of low-cost production technologies and sharing platforms, fans of many other franchises such as *Harry Potter* or *Game of Thrones* create dozens of alternative versions, parallel stories, and parodies. For example, individuals can reinterpret a famous singer's video clip for satirical or political purposes, and then publish their own version on platforms like YouTube.

Sometimes, active fan participation can come to represent a problem for the cultural industry. Copyright can be a major factor of clashes between fans and industry. Fans tend not to accept rigid forms of copyright management and can feel entitled to violate it in the name of their right to invent and tell stories related to the original cultural product. In the case of *Star Wars*, the approach has been traditionally flexible: the original producer, Lucas Film, used to run a platform for fans to exchange their productions, so that they could create alternative stories while giving the industry control over possible profits. For example, *Star Wars Uncut* is a parody remake of two films in the *Star Wars* series. Its uniqueness is that it was produced by splitting the original film into small sections of 15 seconds each, and then asking fans to reshoot one of the resulting scenes in any way. A software would then reconstruct the film, which therefore is a fun patchwork of surprising and different styles and genres. The first movie in the series, produced in 2010, was independent from the owner of the franchise but tolerated from the point of view of copyright as long as it was not used to generate profits. Later, Disney included it in the content of its starwars.com website and in 2014, the second movie was released on the franchise's official YouTube channel (Truitt 2014). This kind of flexibility is important. An active and dynamic fan base helps retain the audience and represents a form of marketing. But it can also provide companies with a pool of information and creativity they can exploit to their advantage. However, different cultural industries follow different strategies of interaction with their publics (Tushnet 2017). Some companies choose flexible and permissive approaches, while others take on "prohibitionist" attitudes and try to crack down on unauthorized fans who revisit or recreate content from their franchises. In many cases, however, cultural industries seek to exploit the phenomenon to their advantage, especially by channeling widespread fan creativity through their own private platforms, so as to encourage production of content and information that can then be incorporated into their products. In these cases copyright assumes the role of modulator of participation, as it is used to control the content produced by fans rather than to prohibit its creation. Understanding this and other contradictions requires a deeper political analysis of online participation and collaboration.

4.2   The Dilemma of Participation

Early research on collaborative media and participatory cultures, especially in the 2000s, tended to paint these collective production processes via digital media as forms of democratization of the media environment, in line with recurrent promises of the information society. However, this idealized vision was soon criticized for its lack of attention to the underlying dynamics of power. The very use of the word "participation" can be seen as problematic. In political theory, the concept of participation implies a redistribution of power to citizens through democratic decision-making processes and egalitarian social relations (Pateman 1970). If we accept this view, however, we must realize that digital media users contribute only marginally to decision-making processes. Indeed the cultural industry and interactive digital services are not fully participatory. For example, authors who have used democratic theory to analyze collaborative media have stressed the difference between access, interaction, and participation (Carpentier 2012). In this model, the simple ability to *access* information through digital media is different from the opportunity to *interact* to exchange or produce content, which happens every time we rate a bar on Yelp or use a hashtag on Instagram; instead, forms of *participation* characterize services such as Wikipedia, whose users may at least partially contribute to deciding about the evolution of the encyclopedia, or decision-making platforms such as LiquidFeedback, used by some political parties to organize their militants. Let us analyze more in detail some of the organizational and political factors that determine the difference between simple content sharing or production and forms of collaboration that fulfill the idea of participation in a collective project (Hyde et al. 2012):

- *Intentionality*: are participants aware of taking part in a partnership and do they share an interest in the collective goals or is the content they create simply aggregated or managed by others?
- *Control of modality*: can users question the rules of participation or must they accept them passively?

- *Ownership*: who owns the result of a collaboration and derives a profit from it?
- *Accessibility*: who can participate and how?
- *Equality*: are there hierarchies or do all participants have equal weight in decision-making?

Analyzing processes of digital sharing and collaboration according to these variables permits a distinction between democratic participation and cases in which the individual and collective work of users is aggregated for profit purposes by private companies, removing power and decisions from the users. The companies that manage services like YouTube, Facebook, or Yelp tend to define their services as platforms not only to describe them from a technological point of view, but also to reiterate that these services are open for users to produce and share content they have created themselves. Indeed the word "platform" refers to a horizontal structure on which one can stand in order to be heard and seen. Through this metaphor services based on user contributions, such as social media or content sharing services, are explicitly presented as neutral and democratic spaces that facilitate horizontal communication. Creativity and participation in collective digital production processes, however, are part of an ideology that is geared toward specific commercial purposes. In fact, most social media companies are based on the exploitation of user-generated content, such as photos (Instagram), videos (YouTube), or reviews (Yelp). Presenting themselves as platforms for free expression and communication is therefore functional to the economic goals of the companies that run these services. In addition, these services use this rhetoric of neutrality to avoid being held responsible for any illegal content published by users, such as pirated movies or hate speech (Gillespie 2010). Platforms based on users' collective participation thus allow the emergence of new forms of collaboration among masses of users for non-commercial purposes, but the latter can also be used by corporations within their business model. In the case of a commercial service such as YouTube, users may retain ownership over a piece of content they produced, but the company has specific rights, for example the ability to couple a user-produced video with a commercial. In a mashup map such as Google Maps, users of Android phones generate the data used to update the map and make it relevant for other users, but their contributions are merely aggregated algorithmically: users have little power over the processes underpinning Google Maps. Processes of data capture and surveillance engendered in social media services mean that users passively participate in improving a platform but do not have the power to decide on the purpose of their role (see Section 5.5).

Furthermore, researchers who have focused on other factors, such as gender, language, or ethnicity, have questioned the accessibility and equality of collaborative media. Anyone can write or correct a Wikipedia entry or become an editor, but this does not mean that the online encyclopedia is perfectly democratic. On the contrary, it is gendered so as to favor male participation (Ford and Wajcman 2017). For example, the majority of its editors, who have veto power on new entries and can ban a participant or remove a piece of content, are white men. Because of this imbalance, Wikipedia has proved relatively adverse to such topics as feminism (Reagle and Rhue 2011). In reaction, feminist groups have organized gatherings where groups of people work together to include new entries on important feminist figures or to correct and expand existing ones. These examples call into question the idea that open technologies and collaborative media per se ensure the development of democratic forms of mediated collaboration. Finally, participation entails a tension between the idea of increased individual autonomy on the one hand, and belonging to a collective process on the other (Kelty 2016). In order to grasp these nuances one must study the technological features of collaborative media, but also critically analyze the deeper political dimensions that shape the distribution of power in collaborative platforms (Carpentier 2016), even when faced with the most horizontal online organizational forms, such as non-profit peer-to-peer production.

4.3   From Free Software to Peer-to-Peer

From the early 2000s the success of a specific form of digital collaboration captured the attention of the social sciences. Definitions such as *commons-based peer production* (Benkler 2006) identify a form of production based upon the free cooperation of individuals as mediated by digital technologies and outside the strict control of private corporations. The metaphor used to define these forms of collaboration derives from computers. Peer-to-peer (P2P) networks are computer networks that are not based on a centralized hub where the information resides, such as a single server. Rather, every computer on the network has an equal role. P2P networks rely on redundancy: thanks to the contribution of many individual computers, the shutdown of a single node does not affect operations, since the same information is available on many machines and can travel along many alternate routes. Using this metaphor, Belgian theorist Michel Bauwens has argued about the emergence of a new political economy of information based on *P2P production* (2005). Bauwens does not refer to a technical infrastructure, but rather to individuals who work in a decentralized, distributed, horizontal manner, without predetermined hierarchies, and share the products of their cooperation. In P2P processes, decisions are not taken by a vertical structure, but rather through the participation of all users.

Box 4.1 Copyleft and Creative Commons

The term "copyleft" is pun between "copyright" and "left." It is a form of alternative copyright licensing that protects the author of a work but also allows anyone to perform certain actions without seeking permission from or paying royalties to the author. Copyleft licenses are designed to remove the barriers to the diffusion and sharing of information created by copyright law. The concept of copyleft was born from an idea put forward by the American programmer Richard Stallman, founder of the Free Software Foundation. In 1989 Stallman wrote the GPL (General Public License) to foster the spread of its GNU software. However, the most popular copyleft licenses are those developed by Creative Commons (CC), a non-profit organization that focuses on licenses designed for creative content such as text, images, or videos.

Those who decide to protect a piece of content, such as a song or a book, with a CC license allow anyone to copy, distribute, and perform the work itself. Furthermore, by combining different forms of the four main clauses of CC licenses authors can choose which additional rights they want to grant to users. The clause Attribution (BY) means that users who run or redistribute the work must indicate the original author and recognize their paternity over the content. The Non-commercial condition (NC) prevents users from using the content to generate profit. The No Derivative Works clause (ND) prevents users from modifying the content. Finally, the Share Alike condition (SA) means that whoever transforms the work and redistributes a modified version must publish it under the same CC license chosen by the original author. For example, a song released under a CC license BY-SA can be played in public, modified, redistributed, and used for commercial purposes by anybody, as long as they attribute it to the original author and distribute it with the same license. CC licenses are legally valid in all respects and have become quite common in some areas of cultural production. Among the most important examples is Wikipedia, which protects its content through a CC license. One of the features of copyleft is its ability to spread virally: as it forces whoever edits and redistributes a work to use the same copyleft license for any derivative work, copyleft is designed to quickly expand in scope and reach.

Although one could cite dozens of examples, one of the best known cases of online peer production is *free software*, the most important of which is the GNU/Linux operating system, born in the late 1980s from an idea by Richard Stallman, a programmer at the Massachusetts Institute of Technology in Boston, and later developed mostly by US and European hacker communities. Free software is based on licenses that allow anyone to use, modify, and redistribute it (see Box 4.1). Unlike proprietary software, such as Microsoft Windows or Apple iOS, which are protected by patents, free software projects make available to anyone the source code, i.e. the text of the program written in programming language. This allows users not only to use a program, but also to study and possibly modify it. The word "free" does not mean that these programs can be used indiscriminately, since they are subject to specific licenses. To explain the meaning of free software, Stallman coined the slogan "free as in free speech, not as in free beer." Free software can be gratis or come with a price. But it is free because it is based on a liberal conception of freedom of speech, that in the case of the software is based on the right to modify, adapt, and redistribute a program. According to Stallman, free software must guarantee four fundamental freedoms:

- The freedom to run the program as you wish, for any purpose (freedom 0).
- The freedom to study how the program works, and change it so it does your computing as you wish (freedom 1). Access to the source code is a precondition for this.
- The freedom to redistribute copies so you can help your neighbor (freedom 2).
- The freedom to distribute copies of your modified versions to others (freedom 3). By doing this you can give the whole community a chance to benefit from your changes. Access to the source code is a precondition for this. (Stallman 1986)

In the 1970s the Unix operating system, owned by the US telephone company AT&T and developed in its Bell laboratories, circulated freely and was open to collaboration. Its source code was available and the improvements made by the scientific community were shared and made available to anyone. Only in 1984 did the commercial choices of AT&T, or rather of the companies into which it was dismembered following an antitrust ruling, change radically. Unix was "closed" and its source code was removed from the public sphere, resulting in long-running legal battles. Following this event Stallman resigned from MIT and began working on an operating system similar to Unix but based on the shared principles of the hacker ethos. The result was GNU, whose name is a recursive acronym for "GNU is Not Unix." While developing GNU, Stallman, and other programmers devoted themselves to writing licenses that would translate into legal terms the ideals inscribed in the software freedoms and therefore prevent GNU's privatization and "closure." They wrote the General Public License (GPL), from which other *copyleft* licenses have been derived (Kelty 2008).

In the 1990s a young Finnish programmer, Linus Torvalds, developed a new kernel, a core part of the GNU operating system, and launched the Linux project, a pun that refers to its origins as an evolution of Unix. Torvalds's intuition was to involve fellow members of the hacker community in the debugging process, that is, the search for problems and bugs in the software. Since then, collective improvements to Linux have made it a flexible product and a direct competitor of the operating systems developed by large corporations like Microsoft. Today, GNU/Linux operating systems are used in the majority of the server industry and a small but significant fraction of personal computers, and are therefore a crucial component of the plumbing of digital infrastructures (see Section 1.4). Linux is also the basis of commercial operating systems such as Google's Android. Over the years, developers who work as volunteers on GNU/Linux-based products have numbered in the thousands and have created dozens of different operating systems, all written cooperatively through dedicated online platforms. This form of collaboration is based on the idea of *forking*: the GPL license used to protect free software allows anyone to "deviate" from the original project and work on their own version without having to start from scratch. Forking has allowed the birth of projects such as Debian or Ubuntu, two of the most popular free software operating systems based on Linux. The history and organization of free software development are often taken as examples of digital collaboration processes. Operating systems based on free software have proven able to compete with proprietary operating systems developed under traditional organizational logics; free software has shown the existence of a new form of collaboration mediated by digital technology; copyleft licenses have created a form of alternative intellectual property which allows collaboration on a digital product or process. Along with Wikipedia, free software is thus considered a successful social experiment in which masses of individuals voluntarily participate in the production of non-commercial technology, content, or information.

These forms of P2P production are underpinned by some technological conditions, but also by social and economic changes linked to the evolution of information societies. According to Benkler (2006), the presence of ubiquitous computers connected to digital networks allows people to collaborate remotely on processes of information manipulation. They represent a physical capital distributed within society rather than, for example, concentrated in factories in the form of machinery. This is based on non-proprietary information-management strategies, such as alternative forms of intellectual property rights that remove the barriers represented by copyright and patents and produce informational "commons," a metaphor reminiscent of England's free pastures before the emergence of capitalism (Hess and Ostrom 2007). In turn, this allows the rise of new forms of horizontal, flexible, and non-hierarchical organizational forms. P2P can increase the efficiency of production processes, in particular due to the low transaction costs of information production and the ability to involve a large number of individuals willing to cooperate in exchange for non-monetary incentives. An important feature of P2P production is indeed its ability to capture and foster the many individual motivations that push people to contribute. These forms of cooperation may also increase individual control over production processes and prove more effective than other organizational forms. On the one hand, users are in control of process inputs: for example, the programmers of a project of free software have access to its source code. They are also in control of the outputs, as they can freely redistribute the results of their work. Other crucial features of peer production are *modularity* and *granularity*. Modularity is the ability to subdivide a project into parts, or modules, that can be developed independently of one another. Volunteer programmers working at a part of Debian need not worry about the whole operating system, but only about the piece that concerns them: for example, the software that manages the webcam, which will be then integrated into the operating system. *Granularity* is the ability to split a task into small sub-tasks. Thus an individual user can provide a tiny or marginal contribution, but that will still be useful for the overall development of the project. Anyone can edit a Wikipedia entry with great ease, for example by correcting a small mistake or adding a sub-section, without having to take care of the entire entry. These features lower the threshold of participation, enticing more people to contribute to the project. Another example is video game modding, a process of user participation in modifying computer games, creating new content, and sharing it online. While most games are proprietary, modders produce new objects or environments that can then be integrated in the main game platform thanks to its modularity (van der Graaf 2018).

Several studies have shown that the motivations that drive people to participate in a free software community or other collaborative and non-commercial processes can be heterogeneous. The desire to participate in non-profit projects, oriented to the creation of use value for a community rather than for private interests, may be part of what some authors have called a new form of "gift economy," in which the remuneration for cooperation is not only economic but also the creation of social ties (Barbrook 1998). This does not mean that free software is an example of a new altruistic economy: programmers who contribute to free software are driven by a complex set of different motivations (Lakhani and Wolf 2003). Indeed, many people participating in forms of P2P collaboration are motivated by the prospect of increasing their reputation, which then serves as a capital they can monetize in other contexts. Among programmers, for example, a good reputation in a free software community can be of great help in finding work and advancing a career. By participating in free software projects, programmers increase both their technical expertise and their authority within the community. Finally, some companies ask waged programmers to devote part of their work time to a free software project. Indeed even if it does not derive an immediate economic reward, the company may benefit from the skills acquired by their employees, which can become useful for the development of commercial products and services. Participation in Wikipedia depends on a set of different motivations too. Content contributions, such as writing or editing articles, tend to be driven by motivations such as learning or personal enjoyment. On the other hand, taking part in the decision-making or management processes that happen behind the scenes tends to be driven by relational factors, such as a sense of belonging to a community (Xu and Li 2015).

It is important to emphasize that these forms of organization are not completely horizontal or democratic: hierarchies exist and remain crucial. Some communities have sophisticated decision-making systems. For example, the community devoted to the development of Debian relies on complex voting systems and has built a formal internal bureaucracy of editors and programmers in charge of major tasks. Additionally, these communities are not immune to imbalances of power due to the prominent role that some members assume thanks to the authority derived from their technical skills (O'Neil 2009). Finally, the development of free software can take place in profit-oriented private spaces such as GitHub, a commercial platform which hosts millions of software development projects and has recently been purchased by Microsoft. Another common critique of peer production is based on doubts about the ability of these processes to produce reliable outcomes, especially when compared to knowledge and information produced by experts in traditional institutional settings. In a book entitled *You Are Not a Gadget*, computer scientist Jaron Lanier (2010) criticized those who uncritically favor the so-called "wisdom of the crowd" over canonical forms of production. According to Lanier and other critics, peer production could foster the disappearance of rational argumentation and obscure individual contributions in favor of indistinct forms of collaboration, in which the role of an individual author can become unrecognizable. As a solution, Lanier has imagined forms of micro-payment that would recognize individual creativity and remunerate each producer for their contributions to a collaborative platform, even when they are minimal (2014). Indeed issues of power imbalance become more pressing if we focus on how peer production and innovation processes are adopted by private corporations and used to generate revenues.

4.4   Open Innovation

Evolved from the experience of free software, *open source* is a movement that, since the late 1990s, has sought to make an open model of innovation attractive to business enterprises, while at the same time avoiding the use of free software's political terminology related to free speech (Ippolita 2005). The success of this model has in fact gone far beyond the volunteer communities that work on non-commercial Linux-based projects, and many companies have adopted open source principles for their products. Yet an episode in the history of computers can clarify how the idea of software production not based on intellectual property rights and professional work was, at first, met with fierce skepticism. In the 1970s Microsoft founder Bill Gates was close to Silicon Valley's Homebrew Computer Club, a circle of hackers and computer enthusiasts which included characters such as Steve Wozniak, Steve Jobs, and Captain Crunch. Bill Gates became the "bad boy" of software partly because of his infamous "Open Letter to Hobbyists," published in the club's newsletter, which complained about the illegal circulation of the software that he produced, the Basic for Altair computers. In the letter, Gates openly accused hackers:

> As the majority of hobbyists must be aware, most of you steal your software. Hardware must be paid for, but software is something to share. Who cares if the people who worked on it get paid? [...] Who can afford to do professional work for nothing? What hobbyist can put 3-man years into programming, finding all bugs, documenting his product and distribute for free? (1976)

Gates thought it was impossible to produce software without an organization paying programmers, and that free sharing would prevent the development of quality software. As we know, however, the history of Linux and free software in general demonstrates that it is possible to develop good non-proprietary software. Free and open source software creates jobs for thousands of programmers, is competitive, and even provides the basis for many successful commercial programs. Microsoft itself admitted it. At the end of the 1990s a series of confidential internal

Microsoft documents called the Halloween Documents were leaked and made public (Raymond 1999). These documents revealed the company's strategies in response to the threat of open source software competition. In it, Microsoft admitted that "recent case studies [...] provide very dramatic evidence ... that commercial quality can be achieved/exceeded by OSS projects." In addition, the sharing of pirated copies of Gates's Basic, which was continually improved and redistributed by hackers, was one of the reasons for its success, as it imposed it as a de facto standard, paving the way for its adoption by large companies such as IBM.

Box 4.2 Piracy and Innovation

The copying and illegal distribution of digital content is one of the phenomena that have changed both the cultural industry and intellectual property rights laws since the emergence of contemporary digital media (Johns 2009). Since the 1990s, tools such as file-sharing networks have made file exchange simple and global. The market for music, movies, software, and video games is affected by a huge amount of illicitly copied content.

Piracy is fought through anti-copy technologies incorporated into digital media such as DVDs, CDs, streaming services or e-books, or with legislative action. Measures such as the US Copyright Term Extension Act extended copyright up to 120 years after the creation of a work or 95 years after its publication. This law was nicknamed the *Mickey Mouse Protection Act* because its approval extended Walt Disney's exclusive rights to Mickey Mouse, which were about to expire. Furthermore, several international agreements have extended the scope and duration of copyright and patents at the global level. Such measures have been accused of not abiding by the original role of intellectual property, that is to stimulate innovation and creativity. Rather, the expansion of intellectual property laws seems to favor the position of those who already hold important intellectual property portfolios, such as Disney.

However, open and informal innovation has an important cultural and industrial role. The term "remix culture" describes a form of cultural production that encourages the cut and paste of existing products, for example samples from rock songs remixed in a hip hop base. This culture is based on the exploitation of piracy or copyright exemptions that allow anyone to borrow, modify, and remix the work of previous artists (Navas 2012). An additional example was the so-called Shanzhai economy, a network of Chinese producers of low-priced shanzhai ("pirate") mobile phones characterized by design flexibility and lack of protection of intellectual property rights or formalized open source strategies. This phenomenon was based on the myriad of small factories that produce components, such as chips or screens, that are then assembled on iPhones or Kindles by other companies. These sub-contractors tend to work in informal networks that bypass Western official producers (Lindtner et al. 2015). China's Shanzhai phones were sold in street markets in Asia, the Middle East, and Africa. They were inexpensive, functional, and linked to a pop aesthetic that played ironically with the stylistic canons of global culture. For example, the HiPhone has the back of an iPhone and the front of a Blackberry. It is estimated that in 2008 the production of Shanzhai phones amounted to 200 million handsets.

Open source principles have quickly spread well beyond the software industry. Today, innovation based on alternative intellectual property rights, open participation, and source code availability are applied in far-off areas such as science, music, or design. In addition, other forms of collaboration requiring direct involvement of individuals in innovation processes have emerged. A well-known case is the sharing of computing resources. SETI@home is an early example of "virtual supercomputer" launched in 1999 at the University of California Berkeley and formed by thousands of personal computers connected to the internet. By installing SETI@home software on a personal computer, the latter is plugged into a network of processors working on the analysis of radio signals coming from outer space. The purpose is to identify any signals from extraterrestrial intelligence. Participation by users who decide to donate part of their computing power is exploited by a software that uses a computer's processor to perform calculations when the user is not active. By aggregating the computing power of thousands of computers, SETI@home has proven able to compete with the expensive supercomputers normally used for these kinds of calculations. Even if they require less active engagement from the user, experiences such as SETI@home are interesting examples of the possibilities created by aggregating contributions from multiple individual users as opposed to more traditional centralized projects. Similar distributed supercomputers have been the model for more recent commercial evolutions, such as cloud computing, that is, virtual computers that use the power of processors physically separated or even located at great distances from each other. Examples are the "clouds" of Amazon or Google, made up of thousands of processors connected to each other in data centers owned by these companies.

Open source has also become a tool for gathering innovations developed outside the company. It is increasingly common for digital media companies to "open" their research and development systems to user contributions in order to improve their products, for example through customer involvement strategies such as online platforms where users can suggest innovations or collaborate to create new solutions that the company will then use in its production processes. This phenomenon is called *crowdsourcing*, that is, outsourcing of a production process not to other businesses but to a crowd of users. This allows businesses to save money as well as collect suggestions and ideas that would be difficult to develop inside the company (Brabham 2013). Scholars have long argued that companies unable to exploit this form of open innovation are destined to realize how a research and development model enclosed within the walls of the company is no longer sustainable (Huston and Sakkab 2006). In the digital media industry an economically important example is represented by mobile phone platforms. The rise of Apple and its iPhone in the 2000s is partly due to the decision to allow anyone to develop secondary applications – video games, services, screensavers, platforms – that can be installed on the iOS operating system. In fact, Apple provides free app development kits. However, the sale and distribution of the applications themselves are controlled by the company through its sales system, the App Store. Google's response was the development of Android, a free, Linux-based operating system that all operators can install on their phones. Android, like Apple, is based on a hybrid model as it does not disclose all its code but provides users with the ability to freely develop applications for the operating system. It also provides users with a relatively simple development environment, which in turn broadens the number of programmers that can produce apps.

Forms of innovation based on open source have expanded and spread to the production of material objects (Anderson 2012), from open source mobile phones to even more complex projects such as cars or biology research protocols. In some areas, these solutions play a commercial role. In design and fashion, there are experiments such as clothing lines whose designs are freely downloadable from the internet and therefore usable and modifiable by anyone. The best-known example of open source hardware is Arduino, a board equipped with a circuit and a controller that can be connected to a personal computer or other hardware. Arduino, developed in Italy by the Interaction Design Institute, is licensed under a Creative Commons license. This means that anyone in the world can download the design needed to build and produce Arduino clones or come up with modified versions. In addition, the Arduino user community has the ability to develop compatible products and software. This has expanded the number of objects that can interact with the board, such as sensors, displays, or motors. The participation of several communities and companies has made Arduino one of the de facto standards in the world of open source hardware. A further step of open source "from bits to atoms," namely, from the production of information to that of material objects, is represented by 3D printers (Söderberg and Daoud 2012). These machines are an evolution of two-dimensional printers and allow users to print out material objects based on designs drawn on a computer or downloaded from the internet – a process called digital manufacturing. 3D printers such as Makerbot or RepRap use 3D files by dividing them into cross sections that are then printed with plastic filaments until they form the final object. 3D printers allow users to produce and share the design of material objects. The application of open source principles to hardware has extended the reach of alternative intellectual property rights beyond software and cultural content. Yet this does not mean that the value produced by digitally mediated forms of collaboration is equally distributed among the producers.

Box 4.3 The Institutions of the Open Internet

The collaborative processes carried out via the internet are guaranteed by a series of technological infrastructures, but also depend on the availability of accessible information, as well as on a favorable legal framework and set of policies. A number of non-profit institutions focus on defending these features and support the openness and democratic nature of the web. Most such organizations are based in the United States and led by charismatic characters – typically white and male – linked to hacker cultures, such as Wikipedia's Jimmy Wales or the Internet Archive's Brewster Kahle. Despite having millionaire budgets and dozens of employees, they are supported by donations. These institutions promote a utopian vision of the internet as a tool for democratization and social progress.

The Electronic Frontier Foundation is based in San Francisco and employs lawyers and legal experts. The EFF deals with the protection of online civil liberties or "cyber rights." Founded in 1990 by entrepreneurs and political activists Mitch Kapor, John Gilmore, and John Perry Barlow, it has been financed by Steve Wozniak of Apple too. Many of its campaigns concern the right to privacy.

The Wikimedia Foundation, based in San Francisco, is the institution that owns and operates Wikipedia. The foundation is not interested in the content of Wikipedia but guarantees the functioning of its technological infrastructure. It also operates other content collections released in open formats, such as Wikimedia Commons (images and videos) or Wikiquote (quotations of famous people).

The Free Software Foundation, founded in Boston in 1985 by Richard Stallman, promotes the spread of free software. It conducts political campaigns against software patents and opposes proprietary software in general.

The Internet Archive is a digital library based in San Francisco that aims to provide "universal access to knowledge." Part of its servers are in the Library of Alexandria in Egypt. Since 1996, the archive has been digitizing books, records, magazines, and other cultural products, making them accessible online, and with the goal of preserving them for future generations. Its Wayback Machine is a repository of billions of internet pages and allows users to browse old versions of websites from all over the world.

The P2P Foundation, based in Amsterdam, studies the impact of P2P technologies and organizations and their role in the transition to new forms of economy. It is directed by the Belgian theorist Michel Bauwens and its website is a wiki which collects thousands of examples of P2P production.

Creative Commons is an organization based in Mountain View, California, founded in 2001 by the law scholar and copyright expert Lawrence Lessig. Creative Commons develops licenses for sharing cultural content and promotes free culture.

4.5   The Economic Value of Cooperation

In the most optimistic visions, peer production seemed to be destined to spread beyond free software or Wikipedia to become a hegemonic form of production which would drive a process of democratization of the information society. In fact, according to authors such as Benkler or Bauwens, these emerging forms of collaborative production would put the means of production – networked computers – in the hands of the workers, together with the ability to control the inputs and outputs of the production process. This would favor the redistribution of wealth created outside the forms of exploitation and private property of capitalism. Furthermore, P2P would represent an increase in individual autonomy and freedom, thanks to the control exercised by users, the dissolution of hierarchies in favor of horizontal decision-making, greater flexibility, and new forms of democracy based on collaborative platforms. Finally, such processes would respond to development goals by providing new information resources to the poorest countries (see Section 6.5). For example, access to scientific data and knowledge and the use of collaborative platforms by researchers in developing countries would be the basis for a more equitable distribution of resources and power.

In fact, free software and other forms of P2P production have spread to key sectors of the information economy and have had a strong cultural and political influence in many spheres of contemporary societies. But they have not superseded commercial production processes that respond to market logics and rely on proprietary forms of information management. Rather, these different forms of information production coexist and are complementary (Birkinbine 2017). As we saw in the previous section, open innovation processes have been adopted by private companies in several sectors of the economy. Free and open source software is also directly used in for-profit services. For example, Google uses Linux within its Android operating system but privatizes its economic benefits. Conversely, hypotheses according to which digital cooperation is guided by a gift economy in which material gains are unimportant ignore the fact that new collaborative economies remain very unfair with regard to wealth distribution (see Chapter 6). In music and software, as well as on platforms such as YouTube or Instagram, few people succeed and make substantial profits, while the vast majority of users receive little or no remuneration for their efforts. This is likely to exclude from participation in the digital cooperative economy individuals who need a material remuneration to survive, i.e. those who cannot count on guaranteed forms of income. P2P technology is used even to produce electronic currency and contracts (see Box 4.4). Traditional forms of accounting for value production in capitalist economies may not be able to grasp this complexity (Arvidsson and Colleoni 2012).

Box 4.4 Blockchain and Bitcoin

Bitcoin, launched in 2009, is the most popular electronic currency in the world. In early 2018 there were about 17 million bitcoins in circulation, with an overall value of about $150 billion. In recent years, an increasing number of institutions have begun accepting payments in bitcoin and the currency has been subject to speculation and inflation. Bitcoins are kept in "digital wallets" that allow anonymous currency transfers via the internet. Bitcoin is not based on an institutional actor such as the central banks that guarantee and control the value of the euro or the yen, but on a computer network that uses P2P technology to ensure the authenticity of a digital object. This is the Blockchain, a public record, or "log," of all events in a system, in this case bitcoin transactions. The log is subdivided into blocks of information (hence "block chain"), which are stored on all computers participating in the system. With a certain interval (for example, about 10 minutes for bitcoins), system information is updated and transformed into a new block that also contains a hash, or a unique numeric sequence representing the previous block. Updates occur on the entire network of users' computers, so no one is able to manipulate the system.

Blockchain technology is also used for other applications. *Smart contracts* are software that automatically perform economic or legal functions. Combined with Blockchains, these programs could be used to organize crowdfunding or manage a mortgage or credit card without a bank. DAOs or Decentralized Autonomous Organizations are algorithms capable of operating autonomously by performing a number of functions without the need for human intervention (Swan 2015). In the future, they could work on the market: an automated car joins a platform like Uber, decides which rides to accept, contacts a mechanic, and negotiates with insurance companies (including their DAO). Blockchains could guarantee the legal and decision-making autonomy of robots or automate legal and financial work by replacing it with public registers: notaries would not be needed in a world where all property relations were available on a public register that cannot be manipulated.

In addition, the flexible forms of production spearheaded by free software have been adapted to interact with the market economy and large multinational companies, for example through phenomena such as the so-called sharing economy. This expression emerged in the course of the 2010s to describe a series of platforms through which people can establish processes for the exchange of goods (such as homes or tools), services (such as car rides or senior care), or knowledge. As a result of the technological success of social media platforms and, above all, of mobile apps, the sharing economy gained strong public visibility. This form of "collaborative consumption" has been presented as a possible driver of economic development, as it generates new businesses and new forms of employment, and as a solution to the social alienation of contemporary societies, as it creates new forms of solidarity and new relational networks (Hamari et al. 2016). This is not an entirely new phenomenon, but rather part of a trend toward a progressive intertwining between productive and consumption activities that people undertake in their daily lives. Since the 1980s the term *prosumer*, which combines the words "producer" and "consumer," has been used to define individuals who have an active role in processes of both creation and consumption of goods (Toffler 1980). Indeed, consumers have long been involved in productive processes: think of the use of focus groups for marketing purposes or the analysis of consumption behaviors to improve how supermarkets display commodities on their shelves. By stating that "markets are conversations," in 2000 the authors of the *Cluetrain Manifesto* provided an understanding of this convergence based on the idea that the internet gives individuals the opportunity to enter into virtual markets where they can actively discuss products, for example by reviewing a book on Amazon.

Companies must take these informed customers into account and stimulate and participate in their conversations (Levine et al. 2000). A more radical approach to this transformation refers to the prosumer as the individual who, while consuming or socializing through commercial web platforms, produces free information that companies can use and appropriate. Interacting with friends on Facebook or reviewing hotels visited during a vacation on TripAdvisor can be seen a form of unpaid work, since Facebook and Trip Advisor's value and revenues depend on the wealth of this user-generated content (see Section 6.3). This model has been criticized as exploitative (Terranova 2000). For example, in many cases the intellectual property rights policies used by these companies do not protect the creators who contribute to collaboratively producing content through their platforms. By agreeing to the copyright clauses they accept when signing up to an online service, users give away many rights to the information they create. In this way, web companies are legitimized to extract revenues from production processes they promote and manage but do not remunerate in any way. Besides private enterprises, however, there are prosumer movements aimed at achieving social or ecological goals: examples of this are local networks of food production and distribution, time banks, or carpooling groups that are organized through digital platforms while allowing the producer/consumer to facilitate the production and exchange of goods and services without serving corporate goals. Indeed, we should differentiate nonprofit and for-profit platforms. Among the former, Couchsurfing.com matches prospective guests with hosts who share a couch or guestroom for free; the "tool libraries" that have popped up in many cities allow users to borrow tools for free; timebanks such as TimeRepublik organize the exchange of favors or services. However, the phenomenon has quickly evolved toward the consolidation of a few multinational companies, such as Airbnb (hospitality), Uber (transport), or TaskRabbit (services and small jobs). In the words of American sociologist Juliet Schor, this sector has been conquered by "corporate giants" (Schor et al. 2015).

While these companies' role in transforming work and the economy will be discussed in depth in Chapter 6, here it is worth mentioning some of their features in relation to the processes of collaboration and cooperation that are central to this chapter. The biggest corporations control vast capital and have market ratings of tens of billions of dollars: in 2018, about $70 billion for Uber and $30 billion for Airbnb. These companies do not own cars or real estate, but use sophisticated algorithms to intermediate, control, and structure transactions among people who have a good or are willing to provide a service, and potential customers. This is not dissimilar from the modular features of the P2P economy, as each worker can decide how to contribute, but the platform aggregates their work into a meaningful and comprehensive service (Kenney and Zysman 2016). For example, an individual Uber driver can decide when to work, but a system of incentives and the aggregation of the work of hundreds of drivers assures that an Uber customer living in core markets such as the downtown area of a Western metropolis will always find an Uber car nearby. More than simply being communities of sharing, these companies are centralized and privately owned market platforms where "sharing" is reduced to the sharing of comments on and evaluations of interpersonal experience, while the economic activity remains structured from the top and dominated by corporate interests.

5

The Public Sphere and Power

Transformations that involve the media system are deeply related to political change. The public sphere, a fundamental component of modern democracies, opens to new practices and actors. In this sphere, the separation between public and private life is questioned, and communications are subject to forms of control and surveillance. The political evolution of today's societies rests on the ability to manage the power of communication networks.

5.1 From Audiences to Active Publics

Traditionally, media and communication studies consider the media audiences as active. Individuals who receive a message do not passively perceive it according to predefined meanings, but rather are able to interpret, evaluate, and respond to it in different ways. If this is true for broadcast media that are distributed from few to many, such as television, radio, and print, within the more complex ecosystems of digital media the public further diversifies. Indeed, media studies refer to a plurality of media *publics* (McQuail 1969). Publics are increasingly important not only in choosing or interpreting media content, but also in the direct production and distribution of such content. Broadcast media such as newspapers or TV channels are based on a centralized, one-way architecture. Decisions on the news or on the information to be reported is taken by a few people who work within a hierarchical organization. The communication travels from one point, for example a television studio, to a potentially unlimited number of receivers that cannot provide immediate feedback. Professional journalists and publishers, as well as companies and political parties, have privileged access to broadcast media, and can therefore reach the public more easily.

Introduction to Digital Media, First Edition. Alessandro Delfanti and Adam Arvidsson.
© 2019 John Wiley & Sons, Inc. Published 2019 by John Wiley & Sons, Inc.

Mass media may be commercial, and thus mainly supported by sales and advertising, but also public or non-profit. In all cases, the system they compose is characterized by processes of concentration, in which the political or economic control of many media channels is centralized in the hands of one corporation, institution, or even a single person. In Italy, the case of former prime minister Silvio Berlusconi's ownership of the most important private TV networks is paradigmatic of market concentration phenomena in television. In Canada, five corporations control most of the market across different media, such as TV, press, and radio (Noam 2016). Digital and network technologies have not radically changed this situation. Yet one of the major effects of the emergence of digital media is the creation of a more complex communication system, shaped by diverse technologies, accessible to non-commercial and non-state actors. This transition both aligns with ideas about the democratizing potential of the information society and generates new challenges. First, digital media increase accessibility: the cost of opening a communication channel, as well as producing and distributing information, is lowering. If in the nineteenth and twentieth centuries the costs required to enter the mass media system (for example by founding a newspaper or television channel) tended to increase, digital technologies provide tools that put media production in the hands of a broader set of actors. Collaborative tools such as blogs, online newspapers, social media platforms, and mobile platforms are instruments that allow the production and distribution of information at a low cost, and make it accessible to individual users or groups that are not equipped with the financial means to start a business in broadcast mass media (see Section 4.1). Platforms for sharing video content, such as YouTube or Vimeo, or photographs, for example Instagram, allow all users to publish and circulate information. These tools facilitate debate through systems that organize comments, rating, and sharing. Through social media and other interactive environments, users can publish, comment on, and share news and information. Platforms such as Twitter or Instagram are paradigmatic of this phenomenon, as they allow individuals to publish texts or images. In addition to the typical dynamics of "friendship" that characterize most social networks, these platforms use hashtag systems to encourage the creation of temporary and ephemeral publics around a news story or theme. For example, all the posts that contain the word "#elections" (hashtags are preceded by a #) are easily searchable by anyone who wants to read news or participate in the debate about that topic, for example that night's presidential debate.

A key characteristic of communications on digital media is that they tend to be organized around a blurring of public and private: participation in public life is based upon the sharing of personal content through individual social media profiles. Thus conversations are neither strictly private nor completely public, but rather assume hybrid characteristics. Connections are built and maintained through the production and sharing of photos, comments, images, and opinions. In this model, collective action seems to be based on shared identities and personal networks rather than on adherence to political ideologies (Bennett and Segerberg 2012). Finally, most of the activities that take place through digital technologies are subject to systematic surveillance. In fact, web companies and governments alike collect information on or retain a copy of most digital communications. These actors are able to determine when, where, with whom, and with which content we interact. Media publics are thus subject to widespread, continuous, and systematic control (see Section 5.5).

Crucially, certain publics do not just produce and distribute information, but actively intervene at all levels of the digital environment: not only on the content, but also in relation to the technological infrastructure of the network, or the software that runs media platforms. American anthropologist Christopher Kelty has dubbed "recursive publics" those groups of individuals that produce and maintain the very platforms they use to actively engage with information and knowledge (2008). An example is a community of programmers working on free software such as Debian (a Linux-based operating system). In order to collaboratively write software these programmers must also design and maintain the infrastructures they use, for example databases and forums, as well as write the licenses used to release their products, and even create the democratic norms and structures within which the decision-making processes through which they choose the evolution of the project take place (O'Neil 2009). In sum, media publics can successfully become politically active thanks to the emergence of an information-rich digital environment and its related communication tools. These changes impact on many aspects of information societies' communicative sphere.

5.2 Journalism and the Public Sphere

Thanks to digital media more and more people have the opportunity to participate directly in the media system, increasing the degree of pluralism while at the same time paving the way for new forms of market concentration. Web platforms and the participatory practices they foster change in depth the role of traditional cultural industry intermediaries, for example in journalism and political communication. Previous positions of privilege make room for an expansion of the public who can access processes of information production.

These changes are the basis of what Yochai Benkler has called "networked public sphere" (2006). The public sphere is the place where people meet for discussion in modern societies. This metaphor includes physical spaces, such as public squares, as well as mediated spaces, such as the press or digital environments. Although the public sphere was not born with digital media, network technologies contribute to its evolution. Political theorist Hannah Arendt (1958) defined the public sphere as the place where citizens gather and act together to negotiate the rules of coexistence. It is therefore an open system that can be accessed and used in a flexible way. Arendt was referring to spaces in the city, but without an independent media system there would not exist a modern democratic public sphere. German philosopher Jürgen Habermas (1984) placed the emergence of a modern public sphere in the Western world, independent of state and religious powers, and based on media such as newspapers, books, and magazines, but also on hangouts such as cafes, in the eighteenth century 1984. In this space individuals that make up civil society are free to discuss politics without being subject to an external authority, and can thus form a public opinion. In modern liberal societies, a rich and vital public sphere is crucial to both the functioning of democracy and the legitimacy of political power. Mass media independent of governments and political parties help create a free public sphere and can monitor the actions of the powerful, a vital democratic function. For example, they can sustain professional journalists who identify the most important issues to be put on the public agenda for debate. However, the concentration of power in the hands of professional information producers (the so-called "fourth power" or "fourth estate") makes professional media a crucial bottleneck of information flow, giving them the ability to filter and direct news. Moreover, their independence from government control may result in an increased influence of economic interests, for example those of advertisers.

Digital media have transformed the functioning of the public sphere, while preserving some of its crucial dynamics. For example, digital media have the potential to diversify sources of information. Individuals have access to an unprecedented variety of sources, including independent, alternative, and foreign sources which can hardly be controlled by state authorities or big media corporations. According to the most utopian visions of the role of digital media, individuals can break free from a public sphere led and controlled by professional and hierarchical structures associated with economic and political power, abandon the political passivity that characterizes the societies dominated by traditional mass media, and assume a direct and active role in the public debate. The networked public sphere would thus provide a wider pool of information and let individuals choose topics of interest and relevant opinions.

Indeed, one of the transformations that characterize the public sphere in the digital age is *disintermediation*, a process of increased independence from professionals who traditionally have the role of intermediary between publics and information (Bardoel and Deuze 2001). Thanks to digital technologies, individuals have direct access to an immense amount of information that was previously the preserve of experts, technicians, or professionals, such as medical information or direct communications by politicians on social media. Also new processes of communication, cooperation, discussion, and public opinion formation emerge as independent of the traditional mass media system. This phenomenon includes epochal transformations of journalism's role. For example, *citizen journalism* is the production and distribution of news by individuals who are not professional journalists and through channels other than those controlled by broadcast communication incumbents (Goode 2009). Among the main tools available to citizens who wish to produce news are social media, but the historical evolution of such tools is worth mentioning. Indymedia, an information site created during the demonstrations against the World Trade Organization that took place in Seattle in 1999, was one of the first successful examples of a platform for user-led publication of journalistic content. Anyone, without the need to be a professional journalist, could post news or comments that were then automatically published and thus made accessible to and commented on by other users. In the 2000s, legacy newspapers gradually adapted to this change, opening online editions in which not only content was made available through new technologies (for example computers, smartphones, or tablets), but also communication started being increasingly focused on the interaction with readers. The boundaries between mass media and new forms of communication thus changed as newspapers integrated online news with interactive systems such as blogging at first, comments and rating later, and eventually moved part of their content to social media. As a consequence, the role of professional journalists has changed. For example, through the use of commercial social media platforms such as Twitter or Facebook, individual reporters can acquire a visibility comparable to that of the newspapers for which they work (Weaver and Willnat 2016). Social media also gradually became sources of information for journalists, as politicians and other actors started using platforms such as Twitter and Facebook to announce decisions or comment on politics (Paulussen and Harder 2014).

A key political function of journalism is *gatekeeping*, i.e. the power to select which news will reach the public and which will not. In today's public sphere, the gatekeeping function is no longer exclusively in the hands of broadcast media, but rather at least partially distributed among users who produce, select, and examine news and information, as well as to new powerful actors such as social media companies. This challenges the *agenda setting* power of mass media, i.e. the ability to dictate the agenda of public debate by choosing the news and topics that will be deemed relevant for discussion in the public sphere (McQuail 1969). Relevant news can now emerge through diffusion on social media and eventually reach online newspapers or broadcast media. In sum, digital tools for information production and sharing allow users to participate in the processes that assess and make visible relevant, as well as reliable and verified, news and content.

Digital technologies also favored the emergence of new kinds of players in the contemporary public sphere. An example is WikiLeaks, a platform for publishing leaks, or confidential information, which has played an important role in the redefinition of the public sphere in a renewed media landscape (Hindman and Thomas 2014). WikiLeaks is an international non-profit organization that collects and releases collections of documents covered by state or trade secrets restrictions. Individuals can submit leaked information anonymously through encryption systems. The organization is then responsible for verifying the documents' authenticity and publishing them while guaranteeing anonymity to its sources. Its goal is to bring to light "restricted official materials involving war, spying, and corruption" for both governments and corporations. The purpose of WikiLeaks is therefore to increase the transparency of governments and businesses through a form of distributed control practiced by all its users. Founded in 2006, the organization became famous with the publication of confidential and restricted documents from Western governments. For example, confidential files on the US prison in Guantanamo; documents published in 2010 revealed massacres of civilians, including some European journalists, committed by US soldiers in Iraq, as well as other cases of abuse and torture; and, during the so-called *Cablegate*, it released thousands of classified US diplomatic service messages regarding European governments and heads of state. To spread these enormous amounts of information, WikiLeaks has worked in collaboration with major newspapers such as *The Guardian, The New York Times,* and *Der Spiegel.* Throughout its history, WikiLeaks has experienced censorship and boycotts. Financial institutions such as Bank of America, Visa, MasterCard, and PayPal have blocked its cash flow, hampering its funding model which is based on donations. Some US politicians even got to the point of publicly demanding the murder of WikiLeaks' founder and spokesperson, the Australian hacker Julian Assange. At the same time, WikiLeaks has received awards for its role in the evolution of free speech. Following this example, similar journalistic initiatives have followed. In 2016 an anonymous source provided the International

Consortium for Investigative Journalism (ICIJ) with a set of more than 11 million classified documents originating from a financial firm based in Panama which provided services for transferring offshore funds to tax havens and thus shield them from tax authorities. The documents, dubbed "Panama papers," involve heads of state and other politicians (Harding 2016). Political information leaks are not new, but digital media have changed their scope by allowing the publication of millions of documents and providing the public with an opportunity to read, analyze, and use them without professional intermediation.

Though fascinating, examples such as citizen journalism or WikiLeaks do not mean than the networked public sphere is inherently democratic in nature. Analyzing the powerful role of private corporations and the new forms of control and censorship that characterize digital media, several critics have pointed out the importance of avoiding representing the new public sphere as perfectly democratic. For example, Zizi Papacharissi has argued that the internet is a "highly privatized public space," rather than an accomplished public sphere (2002). Political theorist Jodi Dean has described *communicative capitalism* as a system of appropriation that resembles a public sphere but is actually subject to exploitation and sur-veillance processes enacted by web corporations, which are the very actors that create digital participation opportunities (2005). In fact, most interactions within the networked public sphere occur on digital plat-forms that are developed, owned, and controlled by private corporations. This has led to new forms of media concentration, as corporations tend to exploit processes of merging and acquisition in order to become domi-nant. These companies take on the role of new intermediaries, and although they have proved able to dent the dominance of traditional play-ers, such as broadcast media or newspapers, they are not necessarily more accessible, open, or democratic. Indeed they can leverage their position to exercise forms of power typical of monopolistic telecom companies (Wu 2010). For example, thanks to its technology for searching information and providing free services (maps, video streaming, news, and countless others), Google has established itself as one of today's core intermediaries between users and information. In a few years its Google News service has become one of the leading global news websites. Similarly, social media have become crucial services used to access political and journal-istic content. For other players, such as newspapers or news agencies, services like Facebook, Twitter, or Snapchat have become the main bat-tleground on which to compete for reader attention. Newspapers are investing increasing amounts of time and money to boost their presence on social media. Inside the newsroom, the figure of the social media man-ager has acquired a central role, while individual journalists have now become social media managers of themselves, and need to support the spread of the content they create for their newspapers (Anderson et al. 2012). Although they circulate content produced by other actors, such as newspapers or television channels, services such as Google News or Facebook implement a new form of gatekeeping, or information filter. Furthermore, this filter function is often outsourced to the service's algorithms rather than journalists. Indeed, the algorithms that underpin digital platforms such as Google News or Facebook shape political and social interactions. These are new forms of "algorithmic gatekeeping," often monopolistic (Wallace 2017). For example, when it was still present on the Chinese market, Google systematically censored information about the events and subsequent repression that took place in Tiananmen Square in 1989, an event that remains a politically sensitive issue in the country. Facebook's algorithms have been accused of playing a crucial political role by presenting selected information to specific users, thus limiting news diversity and immersing us in so-called "filter bubbles" (see Box 5.1). These new intermediaries are commercial enterprises driven by profit. They are not neutral but, as most players in the world of mass media, express specific worldviews, values, and interests.

Box 5.1 Filter Bubbles

What if, instead of fostering open and democratic discussion, social media reinforced prior political views by selectively exposing users to political content they already agree with? Some scholars have wondered whether the internet functions as an *echo chamber* where political orientation is simply reaffirmed. During the US presidential campaign of 2016 several commentators blamed Facebook for how its algorithms select the content each user is exposed to in their newsfeeds. Indeed algorithms try to predict which content a user may be interested in based on their friends and interactions. Commentators argued that social media were producing so-called *filter bubbles*, comfort zones in which conservatives are only exposed to conservative opinions and progressives to progressive opinions. Is this true? A study by researchers at Facebook evaluated the newsfeeds of 10 million users and calculated what proportion of the news stories shared by these users reflected a perspective other than their own (for example, a liberal sharing a news story with a primarily conservative perspective). The study found that algorithms are only partially responsible for creating an echo chamber. Users tend to engage more with stories shared by like-minded friends or posted by news sources they agree with. Facebook's algorithm worsens the echo chamber, but does not create it (Bakshy et al. 2015). People tend to prefer information that reinforces partisan sources over that which includes different voices.

In another study, an analysis of 200 000 tweets measured political homophily and concluded that the presence of an echo chamber depends on how we study it. If we focus on Twitter as a social media we find high levels of homophily (users tend to interact with like-minded people); but if we focus on it as a news medium, homophily is lower and we are exposed to cross-cutting content (users tend to read diverse news sources). The authors concluded that the primary driver of the digital echo chamber is the actions of users – who we connect with online and which stories we click on – rather than the choices the newsfeed algorithm makes on our behalf (Colleoni et al. 2014). In sum, socio-political and technological factors are both present. In fact, and not surprisingly, political content is especially polarizing. A study that evaluated the consumption patterns of iTunes users who were shown personalized content recommendations measured the presence of an echo chamber. The researchers found that the recommendations provided by the algorithm fostered users to listen to new genres and bands and thus overlap more with other users, rather than closing them inside a bubble. In short, there was no evidence for an echo chamber on iTunes (Hosanagar et al. 2014). Musical and political polarization are different, and we tend to be more flexible when it comes to music than with our political ideas.

Finally, both old and new power dynamics are in place. Traditional obstacles to the realization of the ideal of a fully democratic public sphere, such as racism and sexism, remain firmly embedded in online discussion spaces. In 2016, the British newspaper *The Guardian* analyzed over 70 million comments left on its website by readers. Among the 10 journalists that were most affected by hate comments and insults, 8 were women, while the only 2 men were black. In contrast, the 10 least affected journalists were all men (Gardiner et al. 2016). Studies of blogs and social network sites have revealed that these spaces tend to favor the polarization of the debate, giving rise to risks of *cyberbalkanization*, i.e. the creation of small and homogenous enclaves that are constantly fighting against each other (Sunstein 2001). For example, research conducted at the dawn of the social media age showed that the American political blogosphere was highly polarized: those who read blogs of Republican orientation generally tended not to read Democratic blogs. The two groups of blogs had rich internal links but were only partially connected to each other, given that bloggers who aligned with one of the two parties tended not to link content from the enemy camp (Adamic and Glance 2005). More recent studies have nuanced these results. A research study based on the analysis of nine million tweets produced during the US 2010 electoral cycle has shown that Twitter users did not align in a simple

Right–Left division, but rather were grouped in five clusters representing different conservative and progressive views. Cross-interactions took different forms: for example, some users tactically "hijacked" hashtags from political adversaries in order to weaken their communicative strategies (Bode et al. 2015). These phenomena signal how the rise of a virtuous public sphere based on open and inclusive discussion among different orientations and perspectives is an idealized view of networked politics, often falsified by empirical research.

5.3 Politics and Democracy

Limiting an analysis of power in information societies to the communication sphere would be a mistake, as many other variables – such as economic or military power – remain crucial in determining the distribution of wealth, political success, or the ability to control people's behavior. However, power relations are now also systematically organized around digital media, the ability to determine who can access them, as well as the planning and management of information flows. This phenomenon has been transformed and strengthened by the emergence of the networked public sphere, but was present before the mass diffusion of digital media. Since the 1990s there has been an increase in the number of citizens who access information and participate in political debates through digital media, while the number of individuals using only other media such as newspapers, radio, or television has decreased. This change is gradual and develops unevenly in different areas of the world and social groups: for example, Western countries saw the emergence of mass-diffused digital technologies in the 1990; many emerging countries, such as China or Brazil, caught up in the 2000s. Differences are present within homogeneous areas too: for example, Italy has experienced a delay in the emergence of a networked public sphere compared to North America or Northern Europe. Indeed, although the internet can broaden citizen participation in the public sphere, access to digital technologies is uneven. With the definition *digital divide,* media theorists highlighted the difference in access to network technologies that occurs between rich countries and poor countries, or between different classes or generations within the same country (Norris 2001). Indeed, in most advanced economies access to digital technologies and services is significantly higher than in developing countries (see Section 6.5). Furthermore, within a certain area the elderly, women, and low-income communities may experience a digital divide in relation to other social groups. Yet these divides tend to be the result of a multiplicity of factors. For example, research on Canadian seniors has confirmed the existence of both a "generational gap" and intergenerational differences in the use of mobile technologies such as tablets and mobile phones. Such divides depend on several technological and socio-economic factors and cannot be reduced to age alone (Jacobson et al. 2017).

The effects of these changes also depend on the type of society in which they occur. Policies related to access to and transparency of information contribute to shaping how power is distributed. Governments pursue initiatives to control access to information, and often are reluctant to foster greater transparency. In authoritarian countries the distributed architecture of digital networks can make the control of information flows, and therefore of the public sphere, more difficult. This difficulty can create room for free speech, as actors such as social movements may be able to use digital media to communicate freely in contexts in which the public sphere is strictly controlled by a regime. On the other hand, these very changes can also give authoritarian regimes new tools to control the population, since activities on digital media are easily traceable and subject to surveillance. Fears of a less controllable public sphere have led some governments, for example in Turkey or North Korea, to restrict access to some digital services within the country. This can have repercussions not only on freedom of speech, but also on economic development. Non-democratic governments, such as China's, tend to exercise a very tight control on information flows. The Chinese government filters unwanted content through its "Great Firewall of China," a set of algorithms and other technologies that select sources and prevent the passage of certain types of information. Users of that country's internet are denied access to a number of websites and online resources, for example newspapers that publish information against the government. Albeit different and less explicit, some of these problems exist in many democratic countries, which may resort to censorship, filters, or other measures that restrict freedom of expression through digital media. In sum freedom of expression and the right to access information cannot be taken for granted, but rather need continuous revisions and negotiations, and are at the center of frequent legal and political battles (Zittrain et al. 2017). As a response, some countries have discussed and implemented initiatives to protect freedom of expression and transparency. Through a series of laws developed in the 2010s, Iceland has set the goal of becoming a safe haven that protects journalists, internet users, and publishers around the world, while at the same time imposing increased transparency to the government. These laws also aim to attract publishers, databases, and internet providers to the Icelandic market.[1] This is a recurring phenomenon in the history of modern societies. In Europe in the past, the role of safe haven for publishing and freedom of expression has been held by some cities, such as Venice in the sixteenth and Amsterdam in the seventeenth century. Thanks to particularly permissive legislations, these cities set themselves against regions controlled by less enlightened governments or subject to a strong influence from the Catholic Church and its list of prohibited books. These cities emerged as the hubs where most of the books were printed for the international market, also thanks to the exploitation of their position at the center of trade routes within Europe, the Atlantic, or the Mediterranean area (Johns 2009).

Political activity is profoundly influenced by the media, as well as by information management systems. If the most optimistic trends saw the networked public sphere as a means of creating forms of direct democracy intended to supplant the institutions of representative democracy, other more pessimistic accounts tend to see it as a reinforcement of existing hierarchies. It is probably more correct to say that digital networks make new and different strategies of mobilization and participation possible, while at the same time providing an even greater power to some political actors. In Western societies, many political practices significantly depend on the ability to analyze the electorate with techniques derived from the social sciences in order to produce political marketing strategies targeted at different media. Political parties develop platforms to collect data on their voters and supporters, collect donations, and communicate political content. In the United States, both the Democratic and the Republican Party run massive databases containing information about tens of millions of potential voters, such as data on demographic characteristics, voting behavior, and even purchasing behavior (e.g. magazine subscriptions). These data allow analysts to assign an individual profile to potential voters and arrange direct information flows through techniques borrowed from commercial marketing.

In the early 2000s for example the Republican database, Voter Vault, was much broader and more detailed than that of the Democratic Party. This was one of the ingredients of George W. Bush's success in the presidential elections of 2000 and 2004. Barack Obama's race for the primaries of the Democratic Party and subsequent victory in the US presidential elections in 2008 is an example of the use of forms of digital-based collaboration for political purposes, as principles of grassroots political organizing were applied to the digital environment. Thanks to a campaign based mainly on online platforms and created with the fundamental contribution of important figures in the world of digital media, like Chris Hughes, co-founder of Facebook, who was responsible for his online campaign, Obama was able to defeat opponents in terms of number of people directly involved in his campaign, funds raised and, finally, votes. Although the practices put in place by Obama cannot be considered the sole reason for his victory, his strategy leaving his supporters free to act and coordinate autonomously, but maintaining centralized control, has been studied as an early example of the political potential of digital environments. The my.barackobama.com site played a crucial role, with 15 million members who used it to organize at the local level for campaigning and fundraising (Castells 2009). A counterexample would be Hillary Clinton's 2016 presidential campaign, which based many decisions on its algorithm, Ada (named after nineteenth-century programmer Ada Lovelace, see Section 2.4). Clinton's staff had promised to make the algorithm public after the election, but the promise was broken after the defeat Clinton suffered from Donald Trump (Wagner 2016). At the same time, independent initiatives can become even more important than official communication channels. In the 2016 Democratic primaries, the candidate Bernie Sanders was helped by Facebook pages such as "Bernie Sanders Dank Meme Stash," which collected and distributed memes from thousands of users, or by organizations such as "The People for Bernie Sanders," which organized independent social media campaigns. In the same electoral cycle, Donald Trump was backed by an array of right-wing groups that used websites such as 4chan (an underground imageboard forum) to produce and distribute memes and other viral content that increased the popularity of Trump or attacked Clinton, his opponent (Goerzen 2017). In both cases, these initiatives mobilized hundreds of thousands of people, more than those involved in the official campaigns.

In Europe, new political parties have adopted not only communication but also organizing strategies based on digital networks. In 2017 in the United Kingdom, supporters of the Labour Party leader Jeremy Corbyn developed a smartphone app to coordinate delegates during the party's conference (Elgot 2017). In Italy, the Five Star Movement uses its digital platforms to create a space in which people with different political backgrounds converge to openly discuss issues of interest and vote on candidates and proposals. Other examples are Podemos in the Spanish state or the Pirate Party in Iceland, a political movement led by an interest in transparency and freedom of expression, the protection of individual digital rights and privacy, and intellectual property law reform. These parties have grown to become major political actors, elected representatives in national legislations and at the European Parliament, and have won important cities such as Barcelona and Rome. They promote digital-media-based forms of political participation. An example is the use of Liquidfeedback, a platform which provides tools for political organizations to implement voting systems that assume that participants have different opinions that should not be overlooked but instead accurately represented. Through such services, any member can post their opinion or proposal, which is then voted upon by other participants. These "digital parties" may signal the emergence of organizational structures that in the future could ensure a vibrant and dynamic democratic debate attuned to the networked public sphere, while representing an alternative to the traditional mass parties of the twentieth century (Gerbaudo 2018). Yet they tend to be led by charismatic leaders who resemble those of internet-based institutions (see Box 4.3). Some authors argue that these forms of digital democracy arise from the success of institutions like Wikipedia, which are based on a culture of participation based on direct access to information and online cooperation (Tkacz 2015). On the other hand, the idea that technological solutions could be the answer to the problems of advanced democracies mirrors hopes that have been present all along the history of information societies, namely the idea that new technologies are per se bearers of democracy (Mattelart 2003).

5.4 Social Movements

If political power lies at least partially in the ability to program and control networks, movements that counter established power or act for social change must base their actions on trying to *re-program* digital media (Castells 2009), that is, use them to communicate their contents and values by modifying their original purpose or finding new ways to exploit their technological and social characteristics. Media that allow digital cooperation and social media are important parts of these processes, since they ensure a greater ability to act independently, are versatile, and interactive. However, they do not replace the role of traditional broadcast media but rather overlap and interact with them. Furthermore, digital media affect political participation, since they lower both the material and symbolic costs of accessing politics. Finally, mediated forms of political participation are often based on sharing personal content on social media platforms. This form of political activism, which has been termed "connective action," has been said to be in the process of replacing traditional forms of collective action (Bennett and Segerberg 2012). Connective action is based on the overlap between public and private that characterizes interactions on social media. These take place through the activation of networks of personal contacts, as well as through the construction and expression of collective identities. According to some scholars, such features have been the basis for the emergence of new movements since the late 2000s (Gerbaudo and Treré 2015).

Social movements have always been experimenters and innovators in the field of political action through digital media. Among the first examples is the Zapatista movement in Chiapas, Mexico, which, after its uprising on 1 January 1994, created a global network of support through the use of independent online media. The creation of a communication system based on Western commercial digital media and thus an alternative to broadcast media managed by dictatorial regimes has been hailed as one of the main weapons in the hands of political oppositions in the Middle East: the 2010 protests in Iran have been dubbed a "Twitter revolution," while the "Arab spring" that created a series of uprisings in Middle Eastern countries in 2011 has been described as heavily relying on Facebook for political mobilization (see Box 5.2). In the West, an example of social movements in which forms of online participation were crucial for the success of street mobilizations are the so-called "Purple people" in Italy, which in 2009 used Facebook to organize and promote the "No Berlusconi Day," a massive rally against then prime minister Silvio Berlusconi. In 2011, both the 15M Movement in Spain and Occupy Wall Street in the United States relied heavily on the use of social media and other digital platforms for communication, organization, and deliberation.

Critics of the role of digital media for political participation have stressed that most online activities amount to "slacktivism" (a pun between "slacker" and "activism"), as users tend to post comments or photos of political significance on their profiles, sign online petitions, or join groups that support this or that cause. All these activities require minimal investment and may not lead to any result in terms of social change or influence over the political process. However, scholars have demonstrated the relation between online activism and political change, as social media can sustain political mobilization over time (Howard et al. 2016). In many cases digital media do not replace street protests or other forms of political activism, but are rather functional to the reappropriation of public space by social movements. Social media are not sufficient to create mass mobilizations but are useful in facilitating the rapid spread of information. For example, in 2014 and 2015 a series of videos of killings of unarmed African Americans by white policemen, often filmed by passers-by on mobile phones and posted on YouTube, has been instrumental in the growth of the Black Lives Matter movement in the United States. Social movements, however, tend to be based on a combination of online and offline presence: it is the experience of being physically together in the street, next to each other, that provides the emotional motivation necessary for people to actively mobilize.

Box 5.2 The Arab Spring

On 17 December 2010, street vendor Mohamed Bouazizi set himself on fire in public to protest against the regime of Tunisian president Ben Ali. This date is considered the beginning of the Arab Spring, a series of popular uprisings that toppled authoritarian regimes in Tunisia, Egypt, and Libya, and sparked violent conflicts in Syria, Yemen, and Bahrain, and other countries in the Middle East. The Arab Spring has also inspired movements such as the 15M occupation of squares in Spain and Occupy Wall Street in the US. Many of the participants to the demonstrations and actions of the Arab Spring used social media platforms as tools for organizing as well as symbols of democracy and freedom (Gerbaudo 2012). In Tahrir Square in Cairo, one of the most symbolic protest sites, the demonstrators even brandished signs that simply read "Facebook." These events created a debate on the role of digital media for social movement politics. The most extreme positions argued that social media like Twitter and Facebook caused and fueled the protests. This was not new: the mobilizations that followed the Iranian elections of 2009 had already been described as a "Twitter revolution." This argument is not strictly technologically determinist. Studies of the role of then "new" media such as Xerox copiers in the collapse of Socialists regimes in Eastern Europe in the late twentieth century (Dányi 2006) have argued that, beyond the technical affordances of a new technology, one should understand its symbolic role in a society. In this sense, by providing new spaces for political debate, both Xerox copiers in Hungary in the 1980s and Facebook in Egypt in the 2010s represented political openness vis-à-vis a closed and regressive regime. However the Arab Spring and other social movements have complex roots, which combine structural causes such as the emergence of a strata of educated middle-class citizens and the consequent growing gap between the younger generations' expectations and their ability to pursue them, and global causes such as the unfulfilled promises of transition toward more democratic political systems in the Middle East.

Still, social media have played a very important concrete role in the Arab Spring. They allowed rapid mobilization and were key for processes of viral communication. Furthermore, they represented an alternative source of information that functioned despite governmental censorship efforts, and reached both local populations and foreign observers. The Facebook page "We are all Khaled Said," named after a young Egyptian whose violent death at the hands of the police sparked indignation in the lead-up to the uprising in the country, involved thousands and created some of the conditions for the 2011 revolt. In contrast, tweets coming from Iran during the 2009 protests were mostly in English and therefore targeted at foreign observers and journalists, who had thus access to information that the regime was trying to obscure (Lotan et al. 2011). Finally, social media represented forums in which movements could quickly articulate opinions and mobilize. The major events that marked the revolution in Egypt were preceded by massive discussions on Facebook.

Mobile technologies have shaped the evolution of these forms of online political organizing. Mobile phones, tablets, smartphones, and other mobile devices allow individuals to increase access to social media and implement new connection dynamics. These phenomena have been studied for their effect on social movements. American writer Howard Rheingold (2003) described "smart mobs" as groups of network users that coordinate collective behavior through mobile devices, while Castells (2009) discussed the emergence of "insurgent communities of practice" mediated by mobile technologies. Beyond their role for the production and circulation of information, mobile media can in fact implement identity formation processes that can be used to create new forms of political organizing. Collective mass actions such as the protests against the World Trade Organization in Seattle in 1999, the mobilization against the Spanish prime minister José Aznar after the terrorist attacks that struck Madrid in 2004, or the "umbrella movement" in Hong Kong in 2014, have been interpreted as examples of actions organized in a non-hierarchical form by involving citizens who were not members of political parties or organizations, and had the opportunity to exchange information in real time thanks to smartphones, wireless networks, and platforms for citizen journalism such as Indymedia in the first case, SMS in the second, and commercial social media in the latter. Mobile technologies tend to have an even greater role in emerging countries, where low-cost smartphones produced in Asia have been critical for the implementation of online communication strategies by social movements.

However, empirical research on social movements that emerged from the 2011 cycle of square occupations in Spain, the Maghreb, the Middle East, and the US has challenged the idea that these movements' use of digital media corresponds to non-hierarchical, spontaneous, or "liquid" forms of organizing. Rather, the use of digital technologies may have created new forms of power and decision-making methods. For example, movements such as Occupy Wall Street were characterized by the central role of the team managing collective social media profiles, such as Twitter accounts or Facebook pages. These groups, which tend to bring together people with both political and technical skills, have been analyzed as a "digital avant-garde" that has the ability to at least partially shape the direction taken by the movement. Furthermore, although they tend to perceive and define themselves in public as devoid of leaders, these new movements tend to maintain hierarchical political roles while not making them immediately visible (Gerbaudo 2016). In contexts of crisis and mobilization, new political activists can quickly emerge on social media. One example is the students who survived the February 2018 Stoneman Douglas High School shooting in Parkland, Florida, and became advocates for gun control. The most visible survivor, Emma González (@Emma4Change), gathered about 1.5 million Twitter followers in two months – an incredible result for a female teenager of color in the contemporary United States.

Digital media also allow the emergence of movements that are exclusively online-based, without opportunities to meet in person, for example during street protests or other events. Among the most well-known examples is the hacker network Anonymous, founded in 2003 within the website 4chan. Anonymous is a network without central hubs, a collective identity that can be used by anyone who wants to mobilize under the group's umbrella (Deseriis 2015). The hacker is famous for its ability to criticize and attack political and financial power. It adopted the V for Vendetta mask, which derives from a famous comic centered on a masked anarchist figure at war with political power. Anonymous achieved global recognition for its spectacular actions, mostly in the form of cyberattacks: against targeted websites, such as Paypal, Mastercard, and Visa to avenge the measures taken by these companies against WikiLeaks; against the Israeli government to protest against the occupation of Palestine; and against the Islamic State in reaction to terrorist attacks in Europe. Anonymous is present in several countries across the world and is based on a network of hundreds of members working in anonymity. Members never meet in person but rather communicate on IRC (Internet Relay Chat), a technology for anonymous chatrooms. Several activists have been arrested and have served or are serving prison sentences. Anonymous has been used as an example of the political importance of the technological and communication skills possessed by hackers (Coleman 2014).

5.5   Surveillance and Control

Political participation via digital media is not immune from the contradictions that characterize information societies. As digital media offer new avenues for mobilization and participation, they also provide new tools for social control and repression. Indeed, digital networks are characterized by a state of "passive participation" in which most information is not in the hands of the individuals who generated it, but rather used by other actors and for purposes outside of user control. Individuals are passively subject to this power, regardless of their political intentions and expectations (Casemajor et al. 2015). Any activity on digital media, whether it is access to a website, search engine use, interaction on social media, or exchange of messages via smartphone, leaves traces that are collected and monitored. User data are in fact recorded, analyzed, and used for purposes of social control or profit. This form of passive participation is created by two distinct but interlinked processes:

Data capture is a set of processes that use information extracted from the analysis of user behavior and interaction to increase the efficiency of web companies (Agre 1994). For example, Google uses user data – from your communications via Gmail and Google searches, to your movements tracked through Android phones – to create consumer profiles and then uses them to present personalized advertising to individual users. *Surveillance* is a process of data collection and analysis undertaken by public or private actors in order to control the behavior of individuals. In many cases, governments use agreements with web corporations to access data on their citizens. While corporate data capture allows the modification and improvement of the user experience, surveillance is covert and not perceptible by the user.

In the 1970s, French historian and philosopher Michel Foucault described the birth of a "disciplinary society" characterized by the pervasiveness of institutions dedicated to observing and normalizing citizens' behavior (1977). To describe disciplinary power, Foucault used the example of the Panopticon, a prison designed in the eighteenth century by the English philosopher and jurist Jeremy Bentham. The architecture of this building allows one person to control all the prisoners, who are always visible but are not able to tell whether they are being observed. Similarly, the modern disciplinary society analyzed by Foucault was based on institutional control over individuals. Another French philosopher, Gilles Deleuze, has proposed that the contemporary era is characterized by the transition to a "society of control" in which power is exercised through continuous and instantaneous control of the population, and even spread in the "brains and bodies" of the citizens (1992). Several authors have referred to Foucault and Deleuze in order to interpret surveillance processes carried out through digital technologies, in particular since the 2010s and, later on, in reaction to revelations about the depth and reach of today's surveillance systems.

In 2013, the American computer programmer Edward Snowden revealed to the world the existence of secret spying programs put in place by the National Security Agency (NSA), a US government agency. Thanks to Snowden's revelations, as well as further information that emerged later, we know that several Western governments, particularly the US, operate surveillance systems that allow them to record all phone and online interactions. These systems are often used without the mandate of a court (Greenwald 2014). Surveillance processes depend on the cooperation of large web corporations, which have access to the data generated by users and capture it to improve their services or provide personalized advertising. Thanks to this collaboration, state agencies can, for example, turn on the camera and microphone of any laptop or smartphone and use them to spy on a person without their knowledge. These agencies have created databases that contain information on all digital communications, and in some cases have access to data about the movements of users of mobile phones with GPS. Thanks to algorithms that analyze the collected data, both web companies and surveillance agencies can construct the "profile" of a user, that is, a statistical extrapolation used to recognize and interpret patterns of behavior. This is the result of corporations' reliance on data capture and analytics as a core part of their business model. In 2018, further revelations about the intertwining of political surveillance and social media commercial interests surfaced. *The Guardian* released the so-called Cambridge Analytica Files, a set of information revealing that Facebook had sold data from millions of unknowing users to a company that used them to influence the 2016 US elections (Cadwalladr 2018). As we will discuss in Chapter 6, the ability of corporations such as Google or Facebook to extract relevant data from any human behavior has prompted social theorists to use definitions such as "surveillance capitalism" to describe the economic systems that sustain surveillance (Zuboff 2016). On the other hand, surveillance is presented by governments as a useful practice aimed at protecting society from criminal or terrorist activities. However, digital technologies have expanded surveillance to the entire population, in a sense making concrete the society of control imagined by Deleuze. The collection of masses of data from surveillance cameras, emails, social media, web browsing, and phone calls is no longer targeted at individual suspects, but rather extended to all citizens. The production, collection, and analysis of big data through digital technologies has generated a new, and much broader, surveillance system (Lyon 2014). Conversely, resistance to surveillance is based on technologies and actions that allow users to not produce data, or to make them untraceable or not analyzable (see Box 5.3).

Box 5.3 Resisting Surveillance

The growing awareness of the pervasiveness of surveillance in digital environments has fostered forms of resistance. While stricter regulation remains the most important way to defend digital media users from privacy breaches, individuals can choose specific strategies to resist surveillance. Some are technical. *Encryption* is based on a set of coding techniques that allow a user to read a text only if they possess its *key*. One of the most used technologies for the exchange of encrypted emails is PGP (Pretty Good Privacy), an encryption system in which two users exchange deciphering keys that are generated for each message and thus are relatively secure. *Obfuscation* techniques rely on the production of misleading, false, or ambiguous information that makes data capture more difficult and less reliable (Brunton and Nissenbaum 2015). One elementary technique of this sort is the use of pseudonyms by users who do not provide their real name to web services. The more complex ones are based on technological solutions. For example, a software like TrackMeNot sends a multitude of random searches to search engines, making the user's real search patterns more difficult to track. Systems like Tor rely instead on a network effect: each computer running this software helps create a complex network of nodes that reroute information and thus mask the true origin of a user who is accessing a website.

Other strategies are political and have to do with individual and collective choices. *Refusal*, that is choosing not to participate in the activities underpinned by commercial web services, may also be a form of resistance to surveillance and other forms of uneven power. In some cases the decision to abandon a dominant social media platform such as Facebook may be a way to assert one's individuality as a consumer rather than a politically oriented decision (Portwood-Stacer 2012). Indeed, the refusal to participate is a known commercial problem for social media business models; sites such as Facebook need to protect themselves by, for example, designing more engaging user relations (Karppi 2018). Finally, in societies in which the public sphere is highly dependent on digital platforms, and social media use is considered a prerequisite to a meaningful political life, forms of media refusal that are not followed by the construction of alternatives, such as so-called "Facebook suicides," may result in marginalization (Casemajor et al. 2015).

5.6   Information and Civic Culture

Is the emergence of forms of political organization mediated by digital tools and platforms the symptom of the rise of a new civic culture? In the past, political scientists such as Robert Putnam (2000) argued that the civic involvement of the populations of Western countries has been declining for decades. Mass organizations such as trade unions have fewer participants, and fewer people vote in elections or participate actively in the life of political parties. Putnam argued that television consumption has an important responsibility in the decline of political participation. However, the relationship between media and political participation is more complex than claimed by Putnam. An objection to his thesis is based on the analysis of processes of online participation, in particular those related to forms of collaborative production (Chapter 4). Publics composed by the aggregation and collaboration of individuals through digital media devote themselves to the pursuit of common goals, whether it is the creation of free software, the development of lifestyles around a brand, or a protest against global warming. These publics may provide a form of civic education, as members get accustomed to sharing, solidarity, and commitment to a common cause. In this sense, online participation is a form of belonging to a collective (Kelty 2016). For example, the free software movement is dedicated to creating software but also to software politics. Indeed it is actively involved in the design of the licenses that govern the production and distribution of software code. These groups tend to have high levels of homophily, since they attract individuals who share specific interests and values: those dedicated to producing free software, or to campaigning for animal rights, will collaborate and discuss with people who have already embraced a set of specific values (see Section 3.4). These forms of activism can exasperate conflicts and reduce interactions with different people, therefore producing a polarization of society. Yet this tendency to interact only with the like-minded is linked to older and broader transformations: for example, individuals tend to live in areas populated by people similar to them. In the United States the number of "swing counties," or electoral districts in which results are not obvious and both the Democratic and the Republican Party have a chance to win the elections, has decreased dramatically, with the effect of paralyzing the political debate at the national level (Bishop and Cushing 2008).

As we have seen, if the political role of digital media has an impact on the evolution of contemporary information societies, this happens through both a redefinition of political freedom and individual autonomy, and an increased possibility for state and corporate social control. Despite their distributed architecture and open protocols, the public sphere mediated by digital technologies is not per se democratic. Rather, many factors contribute to defining the potential uses and effects of digital media. Will the development of the information society thus move toward a greater democratization? It is an open question, and the response depends on technological, but especially political and social, factors. For example, the network structure of digital media may change hierarchies but does not make them disappear. Well-known studies have shown that many networks are composed of a low number of nodes with many connections, and many nodes with very low connections to other nodes. The latter are unlikely to receive attention from many network users. In his influential work, physicist Albert-Laszlo Barabasi described a complete absence of democracy, impartiality, and equality in a number of networks, from the internet to networks of trade (2002). Because the new nodes in a network tend to connect to those that are already linked to many others, scholars have argued about the presence of a "Matthew effect" in which powerful nodes keep on accumulating connections. The expression refers to a line in Matthew's Gospel: "Who hath shall be given. To those who have not, it will be taken away even what little he has." For example, influential Twitter users such as celebrities or important journalists attract thousands of followers. But this is an uneven process, as in turn most of those users will not increase their influence by growing their own base of followers.

Platforms for participatory information production affect only partially the relationship between media professionals, politics, and citizens. As discussed in Chapter 4, the democratization of information is not the end goal of social media companies, but rather a strategy of public legitimization. Still, rhetorics stressing the democratic role of digital media are part of a longer history of computing: in the past, some important players in the technological evolution of computers were driven by specific political purposes, which in turn have at least partly determined the architecture of the technologies we use today, from smartphones to network protocols (Chapter 2). Web corporations tend to use a rhetoric of liberation and democratization to position their services in a specific political and economic context.

Note

1 https://en.immi.is/about-immi.

6

Work and Economy

The information economy is a dynamic economic sector, dominated by new players. Digital technologies have changed the organization of production and have contributed to transforming labor and consumption. Yet access to the information economy is not homogeneous, and phenomena such as concentration and monopolies are at play. Inequalities between the poorest and richest regions of the world have not disappeared.

6.1 The Rise of Digital Capitalism

The success of companies that produce and manage digital technologies or services is immense. The magnates of the digital economy, such as Microsoft's Bill Gates, Amazon's Jeff Bezos, Facebook's Mark Zuckerberg, and Oracle's Larry Ellison are among the wealthiest individuals in the world, and in some cases the value of their companies has exceeded even that of global oil corporations. According to estimates, in early 2018 Google, Amazon, and Apple had a market value of more than $700 billion each, followed by Microsoft and Facebook at respectively about $600 and $400 billion. The relevance of these businesses transcends their technological or communicative dimension. Web giants are so rich as to influence the development of global capitalism through their investments. For example, in 2009 Google founded GV (Google Ventures), a fund investing at a billion-dollar scale in sectors such as biotechnology, transportation, and hardware. This economic power is combined with the ability to participate in the evolution of the dominant ideologies that underpin Western societies. Bill Gates himself talked about a "frictionless capitalism" mediated by digital technologies, in which free flows of capital, information, goods, and labor are not hindered by regulations or borders. In a sense the kind of capitalism advocated by Gates would be

Introduction to Digital Media, First Edition. Alessandro Delfanti and Adam Arvidsson.
© 2019 John Wiley & Sons, Inc. Published 2019 by John Wiley & Sons, Inc.

based on the fusion of technocratic and liberal ideals, and corresponds to the project of a fully capitalist information society in which barriers to free enterprise are overcome through the deregulation of labor and financial markets, the weakening of nation-states, and the evolution of digital technologies.

In recent years a growing number of authors have reacted to these phenomena by trying to provide a general theoretical framework that encompasses digital economy and labor as part of a new type of capitalist society. Many well-established theories are based on Marxist approaches and build upon the wave of studies of the emergence of an information economy or post-Fordist society that have appeared in the second half of the twentieth century (see Section 2.3). The theories on the transformation toward *digital capitalism* (Schiller 2000; Dyer-Witheford 2015) represent an attempt at explaining the evolution of information societies in a phase in which the ground for comprehensive theories seems to be unstable and subject to sudden changes. Many authors have focused on the financial turn of the economy that has caused the global financial crisis in 2008: the cycles of capitalism are in fact subject to crises in which financial markets acquire relevance until a new productive paradigm emerges (Arrighi 1994). Attempts to define a new paradigm emerging in the present day have focused on corporations' power to organize highly distributed productive processes and even take advantage of human communicative and cognitive abilities. With the definition *platform capitalism* some scholars have emphasized how contemporary capital uses web platforms to organize productive processes based on social cooperation and extract a profit from networked individuals (Kenney and Zysman 2016; Srnicek 2016). These theories are built on the study of digital platforms such as Amazon, Uber, and Deliveroo, and argue that their model is increasingly broadening to influence large sectors of global capitalism. But the role of digital platforms as tools for organizing labor and extracting profits is part of a broader change that has characterized the emergence of information societies, that is, the shift from processes of material production to those based on the creation, circulation, and control of information. Many of platform capitalism's companies do not own anything but a web service that connects producers and customers, and they profit from their ability to foster and control such connections, as well as from a position of monopoly. Other scholars have depicted the birth of a *communicative capitalism* in which affective and communicative skills are the main elements of capitalist production (Dean 2005). In this model, communication activities are commodified and their main feature is the circulation in spaces mediated by digital technologies rather than their content. Some of these theorists are influenced by the famous "fragment on machines," written in the mid-nineteenth century, in which

Karl Marx predicted that emerging forms of automation would liberate humanity from work (1993). Yet the technologies developed by digital capitalism are not neutral but rather designed and adopted to tame and control human labor and extract value from it.

Digital capitalism evolves out of older forms of industrial capitalism and media industries. But it has also shown it has the ability to change by co-opting forms of alternative production. For example, many "creative" companies shape their workplaces as to be indistinguishable from recreational settings, exploit open source repositories for internal information sharing, and organize the workforce in open and flexible teams. Non-profit P2P institutions such as free software communities or Wikipedia would thus provide a "cultural infrastructure" that exposes workers to the kind of social and cooperative production that takes place in web enterprises (Turner 2009). The best-known example is Google, whose Silicon Valley headquarters, the Googleplex, provides its workers with entertainment, open spaces for collaboration, and shared information resources. Google employees can dedicate 20% of their labor time to pursuing personal projects that have not been commissioned by the company's management: many Google services, such as Google News, have been developed in this space of autonomy. Countercultures are co-opted too, as alternative technologies or organizational practices developed by hacker communities provide a source of ideas for digital capitalism (Delfanti and Söderberg 2018). For example, hackatons are design-centered events traditionally used by hacker groups to collectively write a piece of software or an application; they are now commonly staged by corporations such as Google or by startups as part of open innovation strategies (see Section 4.4); independent hacker media such as Internet Relay Chat (IRC), an early text-only chat technology, have inspired commercial social media such as Twitter or Slack.

This chapter will begin with an analysis of the main economic models of digital capitalism. Then it will move to the impact of digital media on the organization of work, the rise of an immaterial economy based on brands and finance, and finally address the problem of uneven economic development in today's information society and its relation to digital technologies.

6.2   Economic Models and Actors

Digital media have a great economic relevance. Digital technologies, such as personal computers, smartphones, digital televisions, or tablets, are part of a global market for consumer products. This market supports the economies of areas that produce hardware components, such as East

Asia or Scandinavia, and others that manage innovation and marketing processes, such as the United States and, increasingly, China. In addition to the market in hardware, digital media have given rise to an economy that is directly based on web services, such as search engines, social media, or platforms for content distribution. Since the mid-1990s, mass consumer access to the internet has unleashed successive waves of investments and new business models that support these companies. On the other hand, technological innovation based on digital technologies has introduced new possibilities and constraints for all companies that produce and exchange information. In many case, this means a deep change in terms of models of production, commercialization, and funding. While the wealthiest companies of the information economy, such as Google, Amazon, Apple, Facebook, and Microsoft, tend to be the most visible in the press and public discourse, digital media have a broader impact on contemporary economies. In this section we will analyze some of the most common business models of digital capitalism.

Some companies simply sell content distributed through digital networks. This was the idea behind the so-called "dot-com" companies of the 1990s, that is that the web was a "content library" that could be accessed by a mass of customers. In the content distribution model, customers can be charged for accessing online content. This business model still exists in some sectors but has become less and less sustainable in others. The arrival of services such as YouTube and Periscope, or social networks such as Facebook and Instagram, has given users new ways to distribute content that they produce themselves. This is an alternative to content produced by cultural industries. In addition, file-sharing systems such as first Napster, then eMule, Pirate Bay, and torrents, as well as video-streaming services, have made it difficult to control the spread and movement of cultural products such as music and movies. For example, in the last two decades the music industry has experienced a collapse of the gains obtained by the sale of physical media such as CDs, which came under attack from piracy, platforms like YouTube, and eventually services specializing in music streaming and based on subscription models, such as Spotify or Jango. The main source of revenue for musicians has reverted to being live performances, while music distribution platforms such as iTunes are sustainable mainly because of the link to the commercialization of expensive technological devices – in this case, the iPod. Other sectors, for example television, have seen the emergence of new successful actors such as Netflix, which sells subscriptions to a portfolio of TV content. Companies such as Spotify and Netflix have been described as working "at the intersection" of content distribution, advertising, technological evolution, and finance (Vonderau 2017). In fact while most of their revenues are based on subscriptions, they also play a role in advertisement and in financial markets (see Section 6.3). In some cases, traditional content providers such as movie production companies form conglomerates with producers of other types of content and diversify their offer by making a movie one object within a diverse and integrated media universe (Jenkins 2006): *Harry Potter* is not just a series of books, but also a number of movies, video games, and comics in which new stories and new characters are developed. Mobile technologies offer a glimpse of the kind of restructuring content providers have been experiencing, as an app used on smartphones and tablets opens up new channels to access paid content. Many newspapers, such as *The Globe and Mail* in Canada or the *Corriere della Sera* in Italy, do not charge for access to their websites via computers but are able to sell content to users of their smartphone app. Indeed accessing content via applications for tablets and phones adds value to the content and is perceived as worth a subscription fee. The book industry is facing similar changes too. E-books for tablets and readers have been gaining market shares at the expense of the printed book and now coexist with older formats. This has opened up new revenue prospects for publishers but also forced them to rethink their business models. For example, they need to find ways to tackle technologies that make the circulation of pirated copies of the books much easier.

The *long tail* is the model upon which giants such as the online store Amazon are built. It refers to the mass of marginal opportunities that digital media can aggregate (Anderson 2004). Instead of selling only a few very popular items, each of which is purchased by thousands of consumers, Amazon generates most of its earnings by selling a few copies each of a high number of items which represent the "tail" of the market rather than its peak. Although each of these commodities produces marginal sales, together they form a mass capable of contributing substantially to the company's earnings. The success of the long tail model is due to the fact that digital networks facilitate the analysis and integration of information, for example by enabling efficient search services for little-known books, and allow the company to accumulate books or other goods in gigantic centralized warehouses. Amazon can do the work of hundreds of small stores, who have to bear high administrative costs and do not have the physical space to store thousands of different commodities, but must instead select only those that sell more. Furthermore, it has the technological and political ability to reorganize the labor process and make it more productive, for example through automation, which contributes to making its prices competitive.

Since the rise of the collaborative web in the early 2000s, platforms which foster user participation through their technological architecture and business models, such as streaming sites, wikis, and social media, have emerged. As discussed in Chapter 4, platforms based on *user-generated content* facilitate user creation and sharing: WordPress makes it very easy to create and maintain a personal blog, YouTube allows video sharing, and TripAdvisor gathers reviews of hotels and restaurants. The economic model of these companies is based on user co-creation (Shirky 2010). TripAdvisor asks users to create the bulk of the content of its website, such as reviews and ratings, that is, votes on the quality of a service or business. Dating services have driven the development of this model: in the mid-1990s, giants such as Match.com were already able to amass millions of ads produced by members willing to pay to access their websites. Many services based on user-generated content have recently adopted a hybrid model. For example, YouTube has increasingly been "institutionalized" through the inclusion of content produced by professionals, such as music video clips or commercials (Kim 2012).

Most services for user-generated content are free to the user and rely on advertising as their main source of revenues. This is the case for social media services, but also for search engines. Both tend to generate and analyze data from user behavior and communications, and use it to provide targeted advertising. The first successful business venture in the field of search engines was Netscape in the early 1990s, but the market is now dominated by Google. Underpinning Google's operations is a software called PageRank. Contrary to earlier search engines such as Altavista, which used human operators to classify the most interesting sites in different categories, PageRank determines the relevance of a site by analyzing links created by web users in relation to certain terms and keywords. Google then produces a ranking in which the website that is higher up in the search results is the one which is linked the most by other websites: since scores of websites about George Washington link his Wikipedia page, this page moves up in the ranking that Google offers to those who carry out a search containing that keyword. This software is complicated by commercial and political considerations, and in fact some sites can be removed from rankings for a variety of reasons. Google also takes into account users' search histories: results can vary depending on who performs a search. In fact, Google is able to offer free services because it uses the information it collects about users, i.e. their search history, as well as information coming from services it owns, such as Gmail, YouTube, Google Maps, and Android, to provide personalized advertising. Thanks to this surveillance and profiling activity, Google's software "knows" (or better, estimates) the age, tastes, consumption preferences, city of origin, and purchasing habits of its users. Thus Google can sell advertising space that targets specific users that are more likely to fall into the demographics or customer base of a certain product. A teenager who lives in Toronto and does searches on video games will receive ads for a new console being sold in Canada, while a business executive who lives in Naples and is a food or wine connoisseur will be exposed to ads for expensive restaurants in her city. Through data capture and profiling, Google and other companies "valorize surveillance," that is, extract value from the pervasive surveillance they operate on their users' behavior (Cohen 2008). In fact, Google is not just a service provider: from the financial point of view it is the largest advertising agency in the world. Through its AdWords service advertisers can publish paid ads on Google search pages. AdSense allows the inclusion of ads on other websites, granting a percentage of the revenue flow to the host: this service is commonly used by websites that base their revenues on advertising (Levy 2011). Social media services such as Facebook follow similar patterns: they invite users to create content that will make the website enjoyable and the user experience interesting, and then sell targeted ad services to advertising agencies, based on surveillance and data analytics (see Section 3.2). This makes online services similar to traditional broadcast media, as commercial radio and television also depend on advertising. However, the advertising market that supports the web economy is different from older ones. Initially, websites were publishing ads the cost of which depended on the number of visitors to the site, just as in broadcast media: publishing an ad in *The New York Times* is more expensive than publishing it in *The Toronto Star*, given that the first newspaper has many more readers than the second. Today, however, more sophisticated models have emerged. With *click-through* systems, advertisers pay a fee based on how many visitors click on an ad and actually access its content. In sum, the provision of free services made possible by the collection of massive advertising revenues represents one of the prevailing economic models of the web. But is it a sustainable model? So far only a few companies have managed to attract sufficient advertising revenue to underpin their market valuations (Arvidsson 2016). At the same time, other partially different models are at play. LinkedIn, a social network for professionals, requires the payment of a subscription fee only to users who want to have access to its "premium" services. Groupon helps consumers find deals and discounts from local businesses and retains some of the money spent on the purchased good or service.

The video game industry has an economic impact not only through the sale of the games themselves, but also because of the hardware market it fosters, for example for computers and consoles (Egenfeldt-Nielsen et al. 2015). Video games are used for marketing and integrated in consumption processes: the video game industry impacts significantly the toy and fast food industries, which use video game characters for marketing purposes or produce games related to their products. Ever since the launch of

Pong, an early video game launched by Atari in 1972 that simulated table tennis, games have been an important factor in the development of digital media. Companies such as Mattel, Nintendo, Atari, and later Sony and Microsoft, have successfully placed subsequent waves of consoles on the market thanks to the success of games such as Space Invaders, PacMan, Mario, Grand Theft Auto, Call of Duty, and Wii Sports. In addition, innovations that are now largely adopted by the movie industry, such as 3D graphics, were in part developed for video games (Bogost 2012).

Finally, *crowdfunding* is a fund-collection system for non-profit projects or startup businesses. Services based on this model, such as Kickstarter, offer the opportunity to advertise projects for which people need startup capital. Individuals can contribute with funding, as these services aim at gathering large numbers of people willing to donate small amounts rather than at large lenders. When the project achieves its goal, Kickstarter retains a share of the raised funds. This system has allowed the funding of a myriad of projects in fields as diverse as music production and technology startups (Belleflamme et al. 2015). In some countries, this model has long expanded to politics. For example, in 2008 Barack Obama's campaign used similar forms of fundraising, relying on masses of small contributions that allowed him to raise more funds than his competitors (Castells 2009).

While the cases presented in this section focus on web-based businesses and models, digital media technologies have a broader impact on the organization of contemporary economies. Indeed, their influence on work, finance, and economic development continues trends that have characterized the evolution of information societies since before the emergence of digital media.

Box 6.1 The Startup Economy

Major web companies such as Twitter and Airbnb are the result of the startup economy, i.e. an economy based on new emerging companies. The phenomenon is closely linked to the development of Silicon Valley since the 1970s and has consolidated around a few shared characteristics.

Most startups are launched by young people and are based on a product, often digital, or on the application of a technology, such as an app, which still does not exist. Many are based on a combination of e-commerce, social media, smartphones, and big data. Startups often pass through an incubator, that is a place that provides a training program in which the company is assisted in the realization of its idea, the design of a business plan, and the preparation of a pitch – a brief narrative that presents the idea to potential investors in a concise and attractive manner.

At the end of the incubation phase, startups are ready to compete for investment.

Some small startups make use of Kickstarter and other crowdfunding platforms to accumulate a small initial capital. In addition to providing financial assistance, a successful crowdfunding campaign contributes to the intangible value of the startup by making it appear attractive to investors. Instead, venture capital funds bet on high-risk private investments, particularly in the hi-tech sector. These funds select a multitude of small startups betting that the few successful companies will realize gains 100–1000 times higher than the initial investments, compensating for those that fail. Usually venture capital "participates" in startups by acquiring a share of their capital, which can be sold in case of success. Because of this logic, a startup's success is not measured in terms of growth on the market, but on its financial evaluation. This value can monetized in two ways: acquisition by a larger company (e.g. WhatsApp was acquired by Facebook for $19 billion) or on the stock exchange.

The startup system is organized around two key concepts that illustrate its position in the digital economy. The first is "ideas are cheap," that is, the success of a startup does not depend on the quality of its core idea but rather on its team. This is why the incubation and training process is focused on giving a desirable cultural form to ideas, teaching teamwork, and brand building. The challenge is not to find the best idea, but rather to handle complex forms of collaboration within a calculable risk. The second key concept is "disruption," which suggests that the best innovations are not cumulative or incremental, but possess the ability to turn entire industries upside down (Lepore 2014). This is the model followed by Amazon with bookstores or Uber with taxis. Paradoxically, the emphasis on disruption can lead to a certain standardization and inattention to people's real needs. In fact, truly disruptive companies are able to create new needs from scratch: no one needed Facebook before its launch. But many startups tend to favor the replication of successful models. Instead of a genuinely innovative diversity, we are witnessing the birth of the Uber for marijuana, the Uber for take-away food, the Uber for laundry, etc.

6.3 Digital Labor and Precarity

Digital media participate in changes in the dynamics of work. In fact, new forms of labor mediated and facilitated by digital technologies have stimulated the rise of a new wave of studies of these processes. On the one hand, these changes are linked to the emergence of new professions directly related to digital media, such as web designer, programmer, network administrator, or social media manager. In addition, existing professions have changed significantly thanks to the integration of computers and networks in the daily activity of virtually every worker, whether it is a doctor who uses the internet to verify scientific information related to a drug or warehouse worker who uses a management software to organize the logistical system that controls how items are loaded and moved. Furthermore, the application of digital technologies to different forms of work and production has given rise to a "cybertariat," mostly composed of workers in low-paid service industries mediated by digital technologies, such as call centers or food delivery (Huws 2014). Finally, consumption activities blend with work, as they occur ever more frequently through digital technologies such as online marketplaces, for example Amazon, which extract value from the unpaid labor of its customers as they review the items they have purchased on the platform. In sum, work in the information economy shifts as it is increasingly organized and monetized through the control and manipulation of informational processes. This shift has resulted in considerable changes in the institutional forms that underpin economic life.

Of course, these changes are part of socio-economic transformations that have impacted the evolution of information societies for several decades. Indeed, the relation between digital media and work has to do with changes in the welfare systems of Western societies, changes in the general organization of work in the industrial and service sectors, the weakening of labor unions, changes in law and regulations, and the rise of multinational corporations which have the power to reorganize work on a global scale (Ross 2012). Furthermore, the use of digital technologies to organize work is not a recent evolution, as the spread of computers and network technologies in large corporate organizations has radically changed the nature of work at least since the 1970s. In white-collar and managerial labor, work gradually shifted from bureaucratic organizations in which each worker had an office and a very specific task, to more fluid, horizontal, and flexible organizational forms. Work started being organized in teams entrusted with completing a task which then dissolve once the results are achieved. The new *knowledge worker* became a flexible individual, able to move from one team to the next, acquire new skills, and cultivate relationships with their colleagues. In this new landscape, special emphasis was put on workers' social skills. These new forms of work organization not only rested on the ability to put to work the workforce's tacit skills, social relations, and shared knowledge, but also required new forms of control and motivation. The management's traditional role in worker command and control was thus coupled with the need to stimulate enthusiasm and passion. The company was increasingly presented as a joint venture that is not merely aimed at profit but also strives to achieve ethical and socially relevant goals. Even in blue-collar work, since the 1970s new forms of organization in factories began to be partially organized in flexible production units in order to increase the flexibility of just-in-time production processes. This change was also made possible by an increasingly widespread use of information-management technologies (see Chapter 2).

This is not a mere technological change but involves political transformations too. As the creation of informational goods and other intangibles moves outside of large organizations, it tends to be based on outsourcing to freelance workers who do not enjoy the security or stability of the previous generation of workers. While in an industrial economy companies were based on a rigid distribution of roles and tasks, in many of today's digital industries different contractual and welfare models based on individualized worker–company relations tend to prevail: workers lose collective memory of rights such as continuity of work, paid vacations, pensions, and in some countries even healthcare, and businesses cut their costs (Sennett 1998). Although companies and politicians may present it as a positive factor which increases independence and freedom for all workers, increased flexibility or precarity has different effects on different types of workers. While for those who have high bargaining power freelancer status can be liberating; however, for those who possess skills that are common, such as web designers or taxi drivers, competition for employment opportunities can be overwhelming (Huws 2014). In addition, the progressive loss of worker rights in areas such as communication, design, and fashion has spread to many other sectors. The loss of workers' ability to act collectively in an individualized market is worsened by the traditional trade unions' incapacity to find answers to new problems that differ sensibly from those of their core base, such as blue-collar workers and public employees. Even welfare systems modeled after the stable labor relationships of the industrial era may be a poor fit for the new needs of the emerging mass of precarious and flexible workers (Standing 2011). In addition, precarious workers often have to face some of the costs traditionally sustained by companies, such as training or travel. For example, the co-working spaces that have emerged in urban areas are a response to the need to collectivize some costs incurred by freelancers working in creative and cultural industries, such as renting an office and purchasing technologies. These costs are thus unloaded onto workers (Gandini 2015). Co-working spaces are offices rented by groups of freelancers in which members pay a monthly or daily fee for access to tools such as a desk, printer, and Wi-Fi network. Initially created by the workers themselves, these spaces are increasingly being privatized. WeWork is a US company that buys property in neighborhoods with significant freelance populations and converts them into commercial co-working spaces.

These new forms of urban labor were captured by the expression "creative class," which became widespread in the late 1990s and early 2000s. It described the new forms of work typical of urban professionals who work in industries such as the production of brands, communication, events, and design. The economy of cities such as London, New York, and Milan has witnessed a rise of such forms of production. According to urban studies theorist Richard Florida (2002), creative industries could thrive in a particular city depending on the presence of a critical mass of members of the creative class. Therefore, his recipe for urban economic growth was to suggest to local governments that they create an urban environment suited to the tastes and lifestyles of these people, for example by renovating abandoned city centers, transforming old factories and warehouses into lofts and apartments, establishing a cultural scene based on a wide range of concerts and exhibitions, and stimulating the presence of restaurants and nightclubs. This idea was thus not only descriptive but also prescriptive, and in fact it has been adopted by declining industrial cities such as Sheffield, Hull, and Birmingham in the UK, which were pursuing a new wave of economic growth driven by art and culture. From the point of view of wealth redistribution, however, the link between creative economy and economic development is weak: urban branding policies have helped to raise real estate value and attract the affluent middle class to urban centers, activating processes of gentrification and speculation (see Box 6.2). Furthermore, some of the assumptions that underpin theories of the creative class have been challenged (Peck 2005). Florida argued that "jobs follow people": if a city attracts talented people, they will create companies and job opportunities. Nevertheless, skilled workers are rather attracted by the local job market, which often depends on public investment in universities and research centers. The most productive members of the new knowledge economy are not a creative class characterized by a particular lifestyle, but rather members of the professional middle class. Finally, the cultural productivity of a city tends not to be based solely on the presence of members of the creative class but also on masses of students, activists, and artists who live poorer and more precarious lives. In this sense, the increase in real estate prices that inevitably follows the transformation of working-class neighborhoods tends to expel the least wealthy members of the creative mass. This has happened in areas such as the Mile End in Montreal, which now hosts video game publisher Ubisoft, or Isola in Milan, with the new headquarters of Google Italy. This is why the promotion of creative cities can be counterproductive. Successful examples such as Manchester or Austin combine low housing prices, which attract artists with little financial resources, with an efficient entrepreneurial environment that can market their work.

Box 6.2 The Digital Economy in San Francisco

For decades San Francisco, in California, has been one of the epicenters of the digital economy. The city is thus affected by momentous economic and social change. The proximity of Silicon Valley and the presence of large companies in town, such as Dropbox and Twitter, have created thousands of jobs and boosted the local economy. But this wealth is not evenly distributed (Rushkoff 2016). The influx of hundreds of engineers (the so-called *techies*), who earn much higher wages than the average, has an effect on the city dynamics and feeds gentrification processes. The pressure of young technology industry workers, predominantly white, and real estate speculation in neighborhoods such as the Mission, historically inhabited by Latin American communities, threaten the local culture. Those who do not work in the tech industry cannot afford rents that have grown unceasingly – in 2017 one could pay up to $5000 a month for a one-bedroom apartment in a central neighborhood. The phenomenon has spread to other areas of the San Francisco Bay Area, such as Oakland or Berkeley.

Therefore, historical and vulnerable populations are exposed to the risk of expulsion from the city, and are forced to move to distant areas and commute into the city to work. The arrival of the techies is symbolized by the anonymous luxury buses used by companies to transport their employees, allowing them to live in attractive urban environments and work via Wi-Fi during the long commute between the city and Silicon Valley campuses. At times, these so-called *Google buses* have been subject to violent protests by the residents of gentrifying neighborhoods. On the other hand, the consumption habits of tech workers have caused the explosion of a service economy facilitated by digital technologies, from apps for home food delivery to Uber, thus creating a large number of precarious jobs with low remunerations, which are mostly taken by women and racialized minorities (Smiley 2015). San Francisco's digital industry has not redistributed wealth, but rather exacerbated some of the existing inequalities that characterize the American society.

In this landscape, forms of so-called *digital labor* have created large areas of outsourced and underpaid work organized via digital technologies or underpinned by web platforms operated by a centralized company (Scholz 2016b), and characterized by the highly precarious working conditions endured by workers in this sector. This can take several different forms. Some platforms organize the work of online freelance workers paid according to the number of tasks performed. For example, a company that needs to contract tasks such as translation, graphic design, or video editing, can purchase the service from Fiverr. The platform is a marketplace that distributes such "gigs" to a mass of workers, who can be paid as little as $5 for small tasks. Any Fiverr worker may decide to carry out part of the work from anywhere and at any time. Other "gig economy" platforms such as Amazon Mechanical Turk (AMT) are based on *crowdwork*: their output is the aggregated result of the efforts of several individuals (see Box 6.4). Workers at AMT or Fiverr are not employees and only need a computer connected to the internet to work for these companies. These businesses are based on web or mobile applications that connect supply and demand and retain a profit on all economic transactions. For example, companies like Uber and Lyft do not own cars and not directly employ any driver, but quickly turned into the largest taxi companies in the world. These platforms organize the work of thousands of independent individuals, who own the means of production but are subject to the company's oversight and profit. After downloading the app, Uber drivers can decide to work at any time but must own a car for which they assume all costs and risks. Uber puts them in touch with customers through its app, decides the cost of each transaction and facilitates it, and keeps a share of the revenues. Airbnb does not own any real estate but has become one of the largest hotel conglomerates in the world thanks to its service, which allows anyone to rent a room or house out and deduct a share of the fee. These companies use digital technology to organize distributed forms of work, exploiting their intermediary position in order to avoid regulations that apply to traditional businesses, such as taxi cooperatives or hotel chains (Kenney and Zysman 2016).

Many gig economy companies also rely on new forms of worker control and surveillance. Work is organized by forms of *algorithmic management*: indeed Uber drivers and Foodora riders never meet the company's management, but rather interact with it only via the app, which assigns them tasks, tells them where to pick up a customer or a pizza, and controls their output (Lee et al. 2015). They are subject to persistent surveillance via the mobile app they use to work, and are pushed to provide a great experience to customers in order to receive the positive ratings that allow them to remain operational within the platform. Their work is characterized by an "information asymmetry," as they do not have access to the information used by corporate algorithms to match customers and workers, decide prices, and calculate a worker's rating (Rosenblat and Stark 2016). Additionally, gig economy companies argue that people who provide services through their apps are not employees. For example, despite the fact that Uber organizes and makes profits from their work, vehicle drivers are treated as self-employed workers who use the platform to get in touch with customers rather than as employees (Srnicek 2016). This has created labor conflicts and lawsuits in several cities where Uber is present. The sector is dominated by big financial capital using its economic and lobbying power to restructure entire markets, for example by competing against the taxi or hotel industry. The success of these companies is also largely based on the presence of a mass of workers who lack alternatives: Uber has become one of the few opportunities for profit and social prestige for the members of marginalized and racialized communities, such as the inhabitants of French banlieue (Chassany 2016); Foodora and Deliveroo offer an alternative to unemployment to urban youth; and Airbnb's great success in Italy is based upon the existence of an impoverished middle class that still owns a second home to rent. Furthermore, forms of division of labor based on race and gender persist or are even reinforced in gig economy platforms. Alfred, a US company which provides workers who perform home chores, mostly employs racialized minorities. This can be seen as the continuation of a long racialized history of domestic service work (Van Doorn 2017). Similarly, a platform such as TaskRabbit sells services based on forms of care labor that tend to be devalued and feminized, such as cleaning, photocopying, or shopping, thus reproducing gender-based inequalities (Sharma 2018).

Companies that follow this model tend to transfer costs such as pension or health insurance to the workers, who are considered independent contractors rather than employees. This model is not only based on technological innovations, but also represents a setback for worker rights and expands precarity and job insecurity to new strata of workers. Theorists of digital labor have described the emergence of a new global working class that does not have access to the system of welfare and worker rights gained in the industrial era (Dyer-Witheford 2015). Indeed, in these contexts traditional trade unions experience difficulties and have so far failed at establishing themselves as forces that push progressive changes in labor relations. On the other hand, new forms of worker mobilization have been targeting some of the most visible corporations of the digital economy. For example, in recent years both the car-sharing industry (Chen 2017) and food delivery companies such as Foodora and Deliveroo (Cant 2017) have been hit by strikes demanding higher wages, predictable scheduling, and better benefits. In response to the forms of exploitation that underpin digital capitalism, there have emerged proposals for the creation of alternatives based on free cooperation. One of these is inspired by the history of the labor movement: *platform cooperativism* is based on the idea that independent platforms and apps owned by cooperatives run by the workers themselves could efficiently organize forms of social cooperation while escaping corporate control (Scholz 2016a).

Box 6.3 Division of Labor at Amazon

The information society, with its networked economy and globalization processes, has not canceled geographical differences and inequalities. Rather, it is based on both old and new forms of local and global division of labor in digital capitalism (Graham and Anwar 2018). Amazon is a perfect case study of the division of labor these phenomena. This e-commerce multinational corporation is based in Seattle, in the United States, but its services are provided globally via its online platforms and a network of distribution hubs in Western countries and beyond. A quick analysis of some of the forms of work it encompasses is revealing of global and local differences that tend to be invisible to the consumer.

Engineers based mostly in Seattle, as well as in other centers in major metropolitan areas, provide the technological infrastructure that under-pins Amazon's platforms and algorithms. For example, these engineers build and maintain the software that runs Amazon Mechanical Turk, a crowdsourcing service based on "microwork" which employs a global online workforce. AMT workers can work for Amazon by simply connect-ing online, and are paid per each single task they perform rather than with a monthly salary. A company that needs to carry out a data analysis that requires human intervention can purchase the service from Amazon. Any AMT worker may decide to carry out part of the work from anywhere and at any time, but the final output will be the aggregated result of the efforts of several individuals. These forms of microwork, which pay a few cents for task, are often carried out by individuals living in countries with low labor costs, such as India. While engineers are recognized as innovative and creative workers, AMT workers tend to be made invisible and struggle to achieve public visibility (Irani 2015). Furthermore, all Amazon custom-ers perform unpaid or "free" labor by contributing to its review system or simply by generating data about their purchasing habits. As in other e-commerce corporations, this information is used to optimize the platform and increase its efficiency (Jarrett 2003).

The commodities Amazon sells are stored in local distribution hubs located in the periphery of major metropolitan centers. Work in these gigantic warehouses involves the material co-presence of hundreds of workers performing physical and repetitive tasks, such as unloading trucks, storing or sorting individual items, and preparing the packs for shipping. These workplaces are managed by algorithms that assign tasks to workers, for example through the barcode scanners used to retrieve items on the shelves. Recently, investigative journalists have reported on the high rates of stress and accidents that are commonplace in these warehouses (Selby 2017). Finally, urban areas witness a different form of labor. In major Western cities, shipping is increasingly organized via app-based forms of labor: through its Amazon Flex app, the company employs urban workers as individual contractors. Anyone can download the app and start delivering for Amazon with their own car or truck. This model mirrors the organization of gig economy companies such as Uber or Foodora.

Similar changes taking place in the cultural economy are not neutral either. Feminist research on the organization of work activities has highlighted the growing relevance of gendered affective and relational labor, for example in areas such as social media management or customer service (Morini 2007). In journalism, for example, the management of relationships with readers through social media, which in the digital public sphere has become a strategic sector, is often assigned to young female journalists who work in precarious conditions (Cohen 2016). Social class plays an important role too, for example in the ability to safeguard one's privacy. Indeed new forms of digital labor also tend to blur the difference between work and leisure. Flexibility requires individuals to work at any time to meet production needs and digital media provide ideal tools to handle these types of requests. Via personal computers, and especially mobile phones and tablets, workers are indeed connected to their workplaces from home, during holidays or while traveling. Leisure time as a fully separate time from work time vanishes (Gregg 2011). Being always connected is a common experience for those who work with digital technologies. Yet the most privileged strata, such as managers, can purchase disconnection services, for example apps that control email or social media usage time, which help relieve the stress resulting from the overlap of life and work (Plaut 2015).

This blurring between work and leisure assumes a specific connotation in other forms of digitally mediated work. While they enjoy the services provided by web companies and social media, users would in fact provide an extremely exploited "free labor" to these corporations, as they collaborate on commercial platforms based on the aggregation of user-generated content, such as Amazon or Facebook. According to Marxist critiques of this phenomenon, such as Italian theorist Tiziana Terranova's (2000), since users are not working under traditional employment relationships, their labor is free in two complementary ways. First, users can freely choose when and what to contribute to a platform. Second, their work is unpaid and this translates into profits for the company itself, which generates value through the content they produce. This can be expanded beyond user-generated content, and scholars have argued that digital corporations such as Google harness "behavioral data" from any activity they surveil via digital and mobile technologies (Zuboff 2016). Even self-tracking devices used to keep track of one's activities and body, such as Fitbit (fitness), Clue (menstruations), or MoodPanda (mental health) generate data that is aggregated and exploited commercially by the platform. Scholars have argued that users of such gadgets and apps should be seen as providing a form of free labor that is monetized by digital corporations (McEwen 2017). On some platforms, labor is unpaid but not voluntary. For example, the plagiarism detection service Turnitin derives its value from the fact that students are required to upload their essays to the platform. Without its ability to aggregate and analyze such user-generated content, Turnitin would not be able to sell its service to schools and universities.

However, ideas about exploitation and value production through online participation present a number of contradictions. The use of Facebook or Fitbit, for example, is very different from waged labor: social media or self-tracking device usage is not experienced as a form of exploitation similar to that experienced by workers. The idea of a linear relationship between value and labor time, on which Marx's theory of value and exploitation is based, conflicts with the non-linear nature of online value creation. It is not the time spent writing or recording a song that determines whether the video on YouTube will become a hit, but other less predictable factors such as reputation and the ability to activate user networks. Finally, the value created directly by the work of internet users is rather small: many web firms rely primarily on their ability to raise financial capital, not on the ability to generate profits. In 2017 Facebook had about two billion users and made about $15 billion in profits on the sale of advertising space. This means that every user "produced" little more than seven dollars per year. At the same time, Facebook had a market value of nearly $400 billion, or about 30 times its profits, a figure several times higher than the average for large multinational corporations. These figures indicate that rather than being based on the exploitation of users' labor, the Facebook model is based on its ability to attract financial investments (Arvidsson and Colleoni 2012). In sum, the size of this exploitation is minimal compared to what is happening in waged labor.

Finally, social media platforms are the sites where a further form of labor is performed. Definitions such as "hope labor" capture the "un- or under-compensated work carried out in the present, often for experience or exposure, in the hope that future employment opportunities may follow" (Kuehn and Corrigan 2013, p. 21). For example, only a few fashion bloggers achieve financial success: think of Chiara Ferragni (@theblondesalad, 500 000 Instagram followers in 2018), Vanessa Hong (@thehautepursuit, 600 000 followers), or Pelayo Díaz (@principelayo, 1 million followers). Yet behind the scenes occupied by these successful Instagrammers, hundreds of unpaid aspiring fashion bloggers perform the labor of maintaining public profiles on Instagram and other platforms, interacting with brands, other bloggers, and their publics, and therefore producing value for the brands of the clothes they wear or comment on. While their present remuneration is exposure and visibility, they hope that their social media activities will one day transform into remunerated careers (Duffy 2017). This is not a phenomenon limited to social media work or fashion, but rather part of the broader diffusion of unpaid labor in creative industries and beyond. The most visible example of this shift may be the rise of internships as a standard gateway for employment in Western labor markets (Ross 2017).

6.4 Immaterial Production: Brands and Finance

In the information economy, value creation shifts at least partially from the production of material goods to the production of intangible goods. In the industrial economy, the central activity, and main source of value and profits, was the transformation of raw materials into material objects, such as cars and refrigerators, intended for mass consumption. In informational capitalism, the centrality of material goods is replaced by intangible resources or assets. This does not mean that we no longer produce material goods. Indeed, the world economy has never created and consumed as many objects and used as many natural and energy resources as it has in our era. However, the ability to produce material goods is quite widespread, and its profit margins tend to shrink. On the contrary, as we have seen in Chapter 2, activities that require information processing skills have become the major sources of value (Webster 2014). This section opens with a discussion of the role of innovation and flexibility in the informational economy, and then focuses on two specific aspects of immaterial production: brands and finance, as well as the relation between them.

Innovation is the ability to continuously create novelties in terms of technology, design, and style. This is Apple's strategy: the company has been able to launch a number of subsequent innovations such as the iPhone or iPad which have changed the way people interact with digital media, or a series of incremental changes, as in the case of the periodic succession of iPhone 5, 6, 7, and 8. Flexibility is the ability to quickly respond to market demands so that the exact number and type of goods is in the right place at the right time. Ikea coordinates a production chain composed of thousands of factories and suppliers around the world in order to ensure that the right products can be found in its shops, which are also scattered around the world, in the right quantities and at the right time. Finally, brands are not only the signs that distinguish a product or company (see Box 2.1), but also represent the ability to generate the perception of a difference between a product and another. Nike is able to create the perception that its shoes are radically different from others, to the extent that in some contexts wearing Nike shoes has become a requirement for social inclusion. In recent decades the weight of intangible assets within a company's market value has grown, and now can account for up to 70% of the market value of large publicly traded companies. Brands represent the most important part of these intangible assets, since they alone account for an average of about 30% of the biggest companies' market value.

The economic and social importance of the brand has grown with the standardization of industrial production. Before the industrial revolution everyday goods were produced locally and in an artisanal way. This made them quite different from each other. The beer brewed in any given English village was quite different from that produced and drunk in the village next door. Industrialization processes tend to standardize products: local English breweries have been bought by industrial consortia that use standard techniques and resources to produce beers that only slightly differ from each other. Therefore, it becomes important to introduce branding techniques that can create the perception that there is a difference between the various beers produced in an industrial way. In order to differentiate their product from other industrial beers, producers need to invest in advertising or sponsor concerts and sports events that link their brand to a certain lifestyle, with its recognizable set of behaviors and values (Lury 2011). Brands are also useful in attracting consumer attention, affect, and creativity. Indeed intangible goods such as brands are increasingly socialized (Arvidsson 2006). By establishing and managing digital environments that foster social relations among customers, companies have the ability to put to work their sociality, knowledge, and communicative and emotional capacities. Until the 1960s, brand identity was almost completely created by companies. This gradually shifted toward advertising agencies. Since the 1970s, however, brand creation relies more and more on consumers. By then, several major brands such as Coca Cola, Pepsi, or Marlboro had opened up to new youth cultures and to cultural ferment that characterized American cities, thus involving consumers in the creation of the brand. In the 1980s, with the arrival of barcodes and the dissemination of credit cards that facilitate the tracing of consumer behavior, companies began to experiment with new strategies of customer relationship management. The core activities related to a brand switched from the aesthetic to the social level, that is, the relationship that the brand is able to entertain with consumers. For example, stores used loyalty programs to extract data and thus predict consumer behaviors and generate enduring ties.

Digital media have allowed the expansion of these practices. Through tools such as blogs or social media platforms, consumers discuss their favorite brands and consumption styles. These "brand communities" (Muniz and O'Guinn 2001) emerge out of a common interest and affection for a certain brand, such as Apple, Vespa, or Hello Kitty. They can arise spontaneously, as a public mediated by digital platforms, but are systematically observed by companies in order to extract useful information that can be used for marketing purposes. In many cases, the company itself creates and fosters the aggregation of communities around its brand in order to obtain a continuous presence in the daily lives of consumers. Many companies build specific platforms on which customers can interact. These spaces, as well as general social media like Instagram or Twitter, are used to organize temporary "brand publics" that generate ideas that can be used in marketing campaigns or even in product innovation, as well as create and maintain affective bonds around the brand (Arvidsson and Caliandro 2015). In Italy, for example, Barilla has launched the campaign "The mill that I want," based on a website where customers can provide the company with suggestions about their cookies, as well as discuss and vote on other people's ideas. These campaigns are important but can also be risky, since they provide users with a free discussion space that is closely tied to a particular brand. In 2012 the website "Space for change" used by Ikea Italy to collect customer suggestions on the evolution of its brand was flooded with hundreds of negative comments related to worker rights in Ikea's warehouses. The website was used as a bulletin board for the protest, damaging the company's image through one of its own interactive communication channels.

The fact that the brand is an intangible asset does not mean that its characteristics are unrelated to the material properties of a product. The experience of the Apple brand is inseparable from the visual and tactile experience of its products' keyboard and screen. Both the way a hamburger is presented and the context in which it is served are part of our experience of McDonald's. Similarly, innovation is inseparable from the innovated product, and flexibility cannot be disentangled from the good or service it produces. Instead of using terms such as intangible or immaterial goods, we could characterize the information economy as being based on hybrid assets, composed of a material level (the material elements of the Macintosh computer, such as screen, processor, and keyboard) fused with an informational level (the brand) to become a single entity. This hybrid quality is reflected in the blurring of traditional distinctions between the manufacturing and cultural industry. Cultural production has assumed a key role in the corporate world, which integrates the production of cultural content and material goods. BMW produces cars and motorbikes, but more than half of its market value is due to its brand's value, which is a cultural artifact.

Another important dimension of the information economy is the financial market. If in the 1950s the US financial market's overall value was roughly equal to the gross domestic product (GDP), today it is estimated as being about 50 times higher than the country's GDP. It is also estimated that the volume of money circulating in global financial markets is about 60 times higher than the volume of money linked to commodity circulation. In addition, the financial economy is integrated with the overall economy to such an extent that it is difficult to analyze it separately. Although this phenomenon is largely due to profound changes in production and credit systems, digital media have an important role in the expansion of finance. Intangible resources such as brands, flexibility, and innovation are evaluated directly on financial markets. In fact, their value is not easily measured through traditional accounting parameters. The production of a resource such as the Apple brand is based on the involvement of a multitude of subjects (designers, consumers, retailers, fans, and managers) and involves networks and relationships that extend far beyond the company (see Section 2.2). A company's brand can legitimize an overall value assessment equal to twice the value of its tangible assets, such as industrial plants, warehouses, and distribution networks. In this sense, financial markets have become very important places for determining the value of resources produced by forms of collaboration facilitated by digital media. At the same time, finance itself has gone through a computerization process. Since the 1970s companies operating in the stock market have been using computers to predict market trends through large datasets analysis. Gradually, the financial market itself has moved to computer networks: the trading pit, which is the area of the stock exchange where financial players physically clash to buy and sell shares, has been coupled to and replaced by digital environments. Indeed one of the skills required of people looking for trader jobs in financial institutions is being a good video game player. Players are experienced in quickly managing complex information flows in a digital environment. Finally, since the 1990s the use of trading bots has ballooned. These are software-based forms of artificial intelligence that are very fast, and can thus take advantage of speed differences of milliseconds (Steiner and Dixon 2012). It is estimated that about 70% of all financial exchanges are now performed by software rather than by human operators.

Box 6.4 Automation and Work

Automation is as old as the industrial economy. In the early decades of the nineteenth century innovations such as the "Spinning Jenny," a machine that automated part of the cotton manufacturing process, increased the productivity of the textile industry and at the same time enabled the replacement of the workers who until then had performed the same tasks manually. A major wave of automation took place in the 1970s and 1980s, when standardized tasks that had been part of industrial production and clerical work were replaced by computerized processes. In manufacturing, many basic processes were automated by the introduction of industrial robots or numerical control machine tools. These machines, introduced extensively in the automotive industry, were capable of performing tasks with high precision and reliability (Noble 2017). In addition, the introduction of personal computers in offices has led to a significant reduction in the number of intermediate managerial levels and professions (often predominantly female) such as secretaries, administrative assistants, and assistant accountants. These processes have reduced both the traditional working-class and middle-class white-collar jobs, contributing to an increase in the unemployment rate. At the same time this loss of jobs has been offset by the expansion of new professions, for example via the growth of specialized jobs related to information management, as well of a "service proletariat" mainly employed in sales and logistics.

Today we are going through a further process of automation in which robotics and artificial intelligence promise to replace not only standardized tasks but also professions that until now have required creativity and human ingenuity, such as communication officers, web designers, customer relations specialists, stockbrokers (robot financial advisors already perform better than humans), and even doctors, at least in the first diagnostic stages. The automation of these areas of work could generate a new wave of unemployment at the expense of the middle class and thus foster new forms of proletarianization in which knowledge workers would join a class of impoverished service workers (Dyer-Witheford 2015). Obviously, this evolution depends on political choices. Fostering entrepreneurship could enable unemployed knowledge workers to create new service companies that could compete on the market. A reform of the welfare state based on a universal basic income could guarantee a decent existence to those who cannot find a job, while a reduction in working hours could redistribute existing work.

6.5   Global Inequalities and Development

Many local and global inequalities characterize information societies, as most resources are far from being evenly distributed (Hargittai and Hinnant 2008). The *digital divide* is the disparity between those who have access to digital media and those who do not. This is much more complex than the possession or not of a computer connected to the internet. Access to a broadband connection, for example, is an important factor that shapes one's ability to participate in digital communication. Another factor is the availability of mobile technologies such as smartphones or tablets. Lack of access to digital media is typically considered a source of social and economic inequalities, since it affects the ability of individuals or areas of the world to fully participate in the digital public sphere, as well as in digital economies based on the production and circulation of information. One of the most visible divides is the difference between rich and poor or developing countries. Indeed some areas of the world suffer from chronic underdevelopment, which is reflected in their access to digital media. This gap also occurs within more homogeneous areas: for example, in Europe there is a gap between Northern European and Mediterranean countries. Similarly, the digital divide can also affect different regions within the same country. In Italy, the north/south economic disparity is mirrored by a gap in access to digital media. The same happens in Canada, where industrialized and metropolitan areas experience higher degrees of access to digital technologies when compared to rural areas or communities in the north. This can exacerbate racial gaps, as indigenous communities in northern Canada suffer from an acute digital divide if compared with urban populations that are better served by broadband and other technologies, and host a more educated population (Haight et al. 2014). In addition to geographical factors, political obstacles can determine other forms of unequal access to digital technologies. Authoritarian countries such as China or Turkey restrict access to online services, often to prevent the diffusion of information that is deemed dangerous for internal political stability (see Section 5.3). Others are subject to choices imposed from outside: this is the case of Cuba, which has had limited access to broadband connections due to the US commercial embargo that restricts its ability to access submarine cables. Finally, the digital divide can be related to the lack of ability to use technologies rather than access them. Cultural and educational factors influence the ability of individuals and social groups to fully exploit the possibilities opened by digital media.

National and international institutions alike cyclically engage in attempts at leveling or "bridging" the digital divide. For example, one of the targets of the Millennium Development Goals that UN member states signed in 2000 and pledged to achieve by 2015 was to increase the availability of information and communication technologies as a prerequisite to expanding the possibilities for even global development. One of the indicators for this target was the number of internet users per head of population. It should be noted that, in the last decade, thanks to the spread of personal computers in Asian and South American countries, the gap represented by simple access to the internet has been declining. However, the most important factor for the diffusion of internet access has been the commercialization and rapid spread of low-cost smartphones in developing countries. Without doubt, the digital divide is linked to economic development. Yet the cause-and-effect relationship remains unclear: is underdevelopment exacerbated by poor access to digital technologies? Or is the lack of access due to structural economic factors? Often, the answer to this question depends on the viewpoint adopted to solve the problem. Most initiatives that aim at bridging the digital divide are based on the assumption that providing more access to information technologies in a poor country or disadvantaged social group will contribute to the reduction of social and economic inequalities. Initiatives such as One Laptop per Child (OLPC), a project started in 2006 under the auspices of the MIT Medialab in Boston, and supported in its early stages by the United Nations Development Program, are examples of this approach. The OLPC program aimed to build and deploy a small and cheap laptop (to be sold at around $100), designed for children in developing countries. The computer boasted special features such as an open source operating system equipped with educational and collaborative software, a case resistant to dust and impact, and a handle to manually recharge its battery. However, the OLPC and other similar projects have had a limited effect on global inequality (Kraemer et al. 2009), while proving crucial for the emergence of a new market for netbooks, i.e. small, ultraportable laptops, in rich countries.

Several development projects are concerned instead with promoting access to information and knowledge, and thus strive to foster literacy and education about digital technologies. Indeed, many think that the development of an economy based on digital media can be encouraged by broadening and strengthening the scope and reach of access to information. The emphasis here is on access to information, rather than just on technology. The expansion of intellectual property to informational goods such as drug molecules, operating systems, or scientific knowledge is often seen as problematic for developing countries, which need to "import" information and cannot afford to pay the royalties that would allow them to access information protected by patents or copyright. This problem could be tackled by fostering informational commons, that is, pools of information that are made freely accessible and facilitate further uses and developments instead of being strictly protected as private property (see Chapter 4). A country that cannot afford to buy Microsoft licenses to run Windows on the computers used by its public administration, schools, or universities may decide to adopt open source operating systems such as Ubuntu, which are free of cost and freely modifiable. Similarly, open access scientific publishing allows anyone with an internet connection to download an increasing number of scientific studies. Thanks to open access publishing, researchers who cannot afford to pay the expensive subscription fee required by traditional scientific journals can access a large portion of the existing scientific knowledge (Nielsen 2012).

However, responses to digital divides that are based only on access to technology or information may not be satisfactory. When analyzing the digital divide one must always keep in mind that the relation between development and technological innovation is complex and multifaceted. According to some economists, development is convergent: it tends toward a greater equality between poor and rich countries. According to this view, poor countries can close their development gap by acquiring technological innovation, which is considered exogenous. Through market mechanisms, a new microchip developed in Silicon Valley can be transferred to a developing country, that can thus appropriate a technology designed and produced outside of its borders. This approach can be summarized in the slogan "chips are chips": there is no difference between potato chips and microchips, since a country that produces the first can export them to import the latter. However, this view does not take into account the difficulties and obstacles that characterize the integration of an external technology into a system, such as sustained monopoly and access issues. According to an opposite perspective, development is indeed divergent, and leveling global differences through technological transfer is quite difficult. Technological innovation is seen as an endogenous factor, and thus its success is the result of choices and investments by local companies and governments, and is underpinned by the presence of a local strata of individuals who are able to drive and profit from technological development (Grossman and Helpman 1994). On the contrary, countries that import technologies from outside are likely to find themselves in a situation of dependence on advanced nations and areas. In fact, competition for technological superiority is one of the main battlegrounds global powers engage in, as made explicit by the technological competition between China and the United States, which has in a sense replaced that between the United States and the Soviet Union.

Hence convergence between rich and poor countries is not obvious, and global inequalities remain despite policies that foster the dissemination of digital technologies to developing countries. New forms of the division of labor on a global scale can even strengthen the difference between centers of technological development and economic power and peripheries that supply raw materials and semi-finished goods. Some areas produce technologically advanced goods but depend on other places for their design and development. Some key economic or technological activities can be concentrated in certain areas for different reasons, often accidental. But once established, these activities are affected by phenomena of *path dependence*: the choices available in a given context depend on the path taken in the past, which is not easily reversible. An example is Silicon Valley in California, which has established itself as a home to hi-tech computer industries and web corporations, as well as biotechnology and energy technology firms. On the opposite end of the spectrum, Central and East African regions have taken up the crucial economic role of raw materials producers, as they can extract material such as coltan, a mixture of minerals used in the production of electronic components, at a low cost (Brophy and de Peuter 2014). In addition, their troubled political and colonial history slows down the evolution of an advanced economy based on technological development. Importing digital technologies into a situation characterized by a lack of technological districts or networks of companies that can absorb and adapt innovations may prove to be useless. Instead, public support of research and development has a high positive impact on the economy of a country (Gilpin 2001).

The idea that the diffusion and adoption of Western technologies could in itself improve the living conditions of poor populations in other countries has been denounced as bringing about an "anti-politics" attitude (Ferguson 1990). Trying to address macro-economic problems, often inherited from centuries of colonial exploitation, through technical solutions instead of political change would thus be useless, or could even reinforce and maintain dependence on rich countries and thus foster new inequalities. The inequalities that characterize the information society are therefore a complex and layered phenomenon that must be placed in the wider context of global inequality and is based on a range of very diverse economic, political, infrastructural, cultural, and social factors.

Conclusion

In an essay written in the early 1960s Umberto Eco (1994) divided the critics of the media, especially television, which in those years was a new and disruptive technology, into two categories: *apocalyptic* and *integrated* (1994). These categories can easily be applied to contemporary critiques of digital media, and indeed re-emerge in many discourses around the social impact of contemporary technologies. For the apocalyptic, new technologies tend to subvert traditional values, strengthen corporate power, alienate people from one another, and generate loneliness and stupidity. Instead, the integrated see digital technologies as a step toward a new modernity that holds the promise of solving humanity's problems, opening markets, fostering economic growth, and democratizing culture and communications. Who is right? Probably both. The information society is not a given, but rather a project that is still unfolding. Its evolution, from the development of "political arithmetic" to the Memex, from the idea of liberatory digital networks to the construction of algorithmic identities on social media for surveillance purposes, is based on common ground: the growing ability to pursue and automate the manipulation of information. Yet the outcomes of such unfolding are still open, and our actions can contribute to the evolution of contemporary information societies toward one of those two poles.

In this book we have tried to stress how, in order to understand and participate in future social, political, and economic changes, we must go beyond our individual experience of digital technologies as consumers and adopt a critical stance that unveils both the ideologies and the vested interests that underpin such transformations. We see this urge as far from being a mere academic goal. As digital media influence all spheres of life, a critical analysis of their significance has become a political priority and requires new and sharp analytical tools. Digital media are a ubiquitous presence in our lives and are changing the way we live together, work, interact with each other, and organize political participation. Many

Introduction to Digital Media, First Edition. Alessandro Delfanti and Adam Arvidsson.
© 2019 John Wiley & Sons, Inc. Published 2019 by John Wiley & Sons, Inc.

factors which go beyond technological innovation are to be taken into account. Indeed, although technologies have the power to influence social change, the direction of that change depends on many other choices and decisions. Political choices and cultural differences shift the balance of the ecosystem of communication which underpins contemporary societies, and this has effects at multiple levels. The balance between the ability to facilitate relational life and create new forms of surveillance and control that determine our experience of social media does not only depend on the design of the platform but also on the political nature of the society in which it is used: open and democratic or closed and dictatorial, for example. As Italian and Canadian television stations have different stories and effects on the two countries, so the impact of digital media largely depends on the social contexts in which these technologies are used.

At the political level, issues such as censorship, privacy, and control are at the heart of changes that in many cases highlight contrasts between transparency and individual rights. Even global politics are a battleground: countries use network and information technologies for military or economic reasons. The emergence of new geopolitical players such as China questions the balance instituted after the collapse of the bipolar world, which was fostered by American technological supremacy. The use of digital networks for political purposes goes beyond their role as organizational and propaganda tools, and includes new forms of social mobilization facilitated by digital media, the spread of new practices in journalism, or new forms of sabotage such as those fielded by hackers. Digital media bring with them new economic models but also affect existing ones. Labor and consumption are influenced by these changes and the sustainability of digital economic models affects the wealth and welfare of large social groups. The emergence of a digital capitalism which organizes work and extracts profit through online platforms creates new jobs while contributing to new forms of social insecurity. At the legal level, clashes revolve around the creation and dismantling of old and new monopolies and conglomerates. The importance of antitrust policies that characterized the broadcast media system is not weakened but, if anything, renewed by the hegemony and pervasiveness of digital media. Finally, there is the technological level. Material resources such as submarine fiber optic cables, or hardware are built and mobilized as new information technologies are developed or adopted. According to a new global division of labor, certain countries assume the role of suppliers of raw materials, leaving to others the opportunity to drive innovation processes based on those resources. The ecological impact of digital technologies invites us to rethink the idea of an "immaterial" and sustainable digital economy.

The form taken by digital media or the decision to adopt some technologies rather than others depend only in part on powerful actors such as governments or multinational companies. Technologies coming from below, for example from independent programmers or social movements working actively on technologies, contribute to modeling and supporting alternative views of digital networks. Consumption practices and user reappropriation also shape our technological future. Clashes around labor rights, environment, and democracy are increasingly intertwined with the evolution of digital technologies and seem destined to play a role in shaping the future of information societies. In this complex landscape, the role of social studies of digital media should not be understated. The opposite visions of the apocalyptic and the integrated seem to leave little room for people's actions. In contrast, we believe that the possibility of actively intervening in the evolution of information societies rests firmly on the ability to critically analyze its technological and political features. We hope that this book provides a first step in the path toward opening up the possibility of a meaningful civic life in our technologically dense environments.

Glossary

Affordances The possibilities and limitations imposed on the user by a technological tool. Technologies can offer new solutions and enable new forms of action, but at the same time only allow users to act in ways that respect the constraints imposed by the technology itself.

Algorithm A set of encoded procedures that use calculations to turn data into specific outputs. Many different algorithms have acquired crucial roles in contemporary digital technologies, and thus have come to influence social, political, and economic processes.

Big data Large masses of data generated by the use of digital technologies. These data enable the analysis of whole populations, but are often owned by web companies. They are also used by surveillance systems for social control.

Brand The ability to generate the perception of a difference between a product and another. In the information society, brands are not simply identification marks, but have expanded to include consumer practices and lifestyles.

Broadcast media Media based on centralized and unidirectional communications that distribute content from one transmitter to many receivers, such as television, radio, and press.

Citizen journalism The production and distribution of news and information by individuals who are not professional journalists and through channels other than those of broadcast communication institutions.

Convergence The process that causes different types of content (written, audio, visual, etc.) to converge into a single technological device. Also, industrial convergence between the cultural and telecommunications industry which makes them increasingly interconnected and indistinguishable.

Copyleft A pun indicating a form of alternative copyright. It is a form of intellectual property that protects the author of a work but also

Introduction to Digital Media, First Edition. Alessandro Delfanti and Adam Arvidsson.
© 2019 John Wiley & Sons, Inc. Published 2019 by John Wiley & Sons, Inc.

allows anyone to perform certain actions, such as copying or redistributing the protected content, without asking permission or paying royalties.

Creative class An expression that describes urban professionals who work in the so-called "creative industries" related to art, information, and digital media, i.e. the production of brands, communication, events, and design.

Crowdfunding A fundraising system for non-profits or startup businesses, based on online platforms that allow the collection of large numbers of small contributions or donations.

Crowdsourcing The outsourcing of a service or manufacturing process to a "crowd," for example a mass of users who do not work within the company.

Cyberspace An expression dating from the first decade of the diffusion of the internet. It refers to the online world as a world "apart," as distinct from everyday reality. In cyberspace people can hide behind fake identities, as in the famous *The New Yorker* cartoon: "On the internet, nobody knows you're a dog."

Digital capitalism An emerging form of capitalism in which value production is based on digital networks and technologies. In digital capitalism, platforms are the key tools for organizing labor and extracting profits. Its flag-bearer companies, such as Facebook, Uber, and Google, are among the wealthiest of contemporary economies.

Digital divide Disparities between those who have access to digital media and those who have not. In addition to access to computers connected to the network, the digital divide is related to the ability to use digital technologies, as well as to social and cultural differences.

Digital labor Forms of work mediated by digital technologies. Digital labor is based on technological as well as social and relational skills.

Digital media A set of technologies and media based on computers and networks. Digital media carry information represented by numerical sequences that they can rework and transform.

Digital methods A set of methodologies for social research that use digital media as sources of data and analysis tools.

Fandom A subculture expressed by a community of fans who share an interest in a cultural industry phenomenon such as a movie, musical genre, or fashion. Fans are often involved in the production of alternative content.

Filter bubble A state of isolation created by exposure to content selected by social media algorithms. Filter bubbles can remove users from viewpoints they disagree with. Their role has been discussed in relation to the outcome of elections and other political processes, as part of the corrosion of an idealized public sphere.

Free software Software whose licenses allow anyone to use, modify, and redistribute it. Free software is based on the open availability of its source code, i.e. the text of the program written in programming language. This allows users not only to use a program, but also to study and modify it.

General intellect The abstract scientific and technical knowledge embedded in machines and based on social cooperation. In the mid-nineteenth century, Marx argued that the general intellect was bound to become the main force of production in advanced societies.

Gig economy An organizational form which uses digital technologies to mobilize distributed workers and extract part of the value they produce. This economy is dominated by large companies that control the technologies used to organize labor and generate profits.

Globalization The growth of global relations and trade. Globalization increases economic and cultural standardization. Digital media accelerate the process and make these phenomena more efficient.

Hacker A group of cultures and communities linked to a set of common values with respect to the relationship with computer technologies. Hacker cultures are heterogeneous and diverse, but share the idea that information should be open and transparent and that technologies should be decentralized and put in the hands of their users.

Influencer Actors that are able to mobilize a large number of other individuals due to the size of the network to which they are connected, as well as their social and communication skills.

Information society A form of society characterized by the prominence of information and knowledge with respect to material goods. The ability to produce, manipulate, and distribute information becomes the main factor of wealth and power. These changes have been described since the early 1960s with definitions that, although using different points of view, refer to the same set of phenomena: *postindustrial society, postmodern society, post-Fordism, knowledge society, network society,* or *cognitive capitalism.* They share an awareness of a historical break from earlier forms of social organization and production.

Intangibles assets Resources not easily measured with classical parameters, but which represent a significant part of a company's market value. Among the main intangible assets are brands, innovation, and flexibility.

Intellectual property A set of legal principles that enable creators and inventors to exercise ownership rights on intangible goods. Intellectual property is a temporary concession aimed at boosting creative and inventive activities. Copyright protects artistic, literary, and scientific creations. Patents protect industrial inventions. Brands differentiate a product or a company.

Long tail A business model based on digital media's capabilities to aggregate a mass of marginal items. This is the model used by e-commerce giants such as Amazon, that is able to sell a few copies of many items. Traditional forms of distribution are based on a few products that sell many units each.

Materiality Digital technologies have specific material characteristics. For example, cables, computers, and other devices are made of plastics and metals. Focusing on these features enables the study of their ecological impact and the role of human labor in their production.

Mediatization Ubiquity of media technologies in the daily lives of individuals. Media technologies' relevance and spread influence social, political, and organizational processes within a society. As the presence of digital media becomes pervasive and is taken for granted, it tends to make them invisible.

Meme An idea that spreads among people in viral form. The term draws a similarity with the gene, a genetic unit that spreads in a population through replication and forms of natural selection. On social media, memes have become a genre characterized by specific aesthetics and languages.

Moore's law A law according to which the performance of microprocessors doubles every 18 months. It was formulated in 1965 and largely confirmed in the following decades.

Networked economy The organization of production processes based on the decentralization and autonomy of production units. Networks are an archaic form of social organization, but information and communication technologies have made them more efficient and competitive.

Networked individualism A form of social relationship that results from the spread of social media. Individuals tend to belong to a multitude of different social networks, often disconnected from each other. In each network, individuals can show or develop a particular aspect of their identity.

New media All media are new when they are introduced, and all new media will become old in the future. However, their increasingly rapid innovation cycles make continuous "novelty" an important feature of digital technologies.

Open source An innovation model based on sharing the instructions needed to produce an informational or material object.

Participation Citizen activity and collective presence in public life. In digital cultures, a "weak" definition of participation refers to the widespread use of technologies to produce and interact with media content.

Peer to peer (P2P) Network architecture with no central hubs. The nodes are not organized as a hierarchy, but rather as equal (peer). In a P2P computer network, each computer can act as both client and server. The P2P metaphor has been used to describe social networks in which individuals cooperate in a decentralized, distributed, and horizontal fashion.

Piracy The illegal copying and distribution of copyrighted content, patented innovations, or branded products.

Platform The elevated horizontal structure that allows organizations or individuals to gain a position of visibility. Web companies describe themselves as platforms to underline their neutrality toward user-generated content. Platforms organize and mediate interactions, and thus shape sociality, work, and cultural production.

Platform cooperativism A movement advocating for the design of democratic and worker-owned platforms. It aims at building a just and equitable digital economy while adopting some of the organizational principles of current corporations.

Privacy The right of an individual to keep out of the public domain information relating to themselves, their tastes, and behaviors.

Profiling Creating user profiles based on their interests, communications, online behaviors, and networks of friends. This information is often used for marketing purposes and to provide personalized advertising.

Prosumer A pun indicating the merge between producers and consumers. It defines users as actively producing content through their consumption practices.

Public A group of individuals organized around a media content or platform. Although not binding for the construction of personal identity, publics offer to their members the opportunity to identify with a common cause and gain public recognition for their contributions.

Public sphere The place where citizens can gather and act together to negotiate the rules of common life. A modern public sphere is based on the media system and is relatively independent from state and religious power.

Recursive public Groups of individuals who are actively engaged not only in producing or using content, but also in building and maintaining the platforms and standards they use. For example, a community of free software programmers who produce code, manage the platform on which they work, and write the licenses used to release their products.

Remediation The process by which new media evolve from and are influenced by previous ones. Video streaming services remediate television through new formats and technologies, but also preserve several of its crucial characteristics.

Reputation What is said about you when you are not in the room. Digital media provide new tools to manage one's reputation. Members of a public acquire reputation on the basis of how other members judge their contributions.

Self-branding The construction of a communicable version of one's identity that emphasizes qualities compatible with a particular strategic purpose, such as job search for a freelancer.

Social media (or social network sites). Online communication platforms based on the formation and management of social networks which allow to maintain pre-existing ties, build new friendships, and interact with an extensive network of contacts. Social media are among the most important actors of the digital sphere: the largest are used by billions of users.

Surveillance A set of technologies and processes for the collection and analysis for control purposes of information about an individual or population. Surveillance is surreptitious, that is, not visible. Through digital technologies, surveillance has become systematic and indiscriminate.

User-generated content Content created by users of a service. Most social media rely almost exclusively on such content for their platforms. User-generated content is underpinned by the unpaid labor of users.

References

Adamic, L. and Glance, N. (2005). The political blogosphere and the 2004 US election: divided they blog. In: *Proceedings of the 3rd International Workshop on Link Discovery*, 36–43. New York, NY: ACM Digital Library.

Agar, J. (2017). *Turing and the Universal Machine: The Making of the Modern Computer*. London: Icon Books.

Agre, P. (1994). Surveillance and capture: two models of privacy. *The Information Society* 10 (2): 101–127.

Anderson, C. (2004). *The Long Tail: Why the Future of Business Is Selling Less of More*. New York, NY: Hyperion.

Anderson, C. (2012). *Makers: The New Industrial Revolution*. New York, NY: Crown Business.

Anderson, C.W., Bell, E., and Shirky, C. (2012). *Post-Industrial Journalism: Adapting to the Present. A Report*. New York, NY: Columbia Journalism School.

Aneesh, A. (2009). Global labor: algocratic modes of organization. *Sociological Theory* 27 (4): 347–370.

Arendt, H. (1958). *The Human Condition*. Chicago, IL: University of Chicago Press.

Arrighi, G. (1994). *The Long Twentieth Century: Money, Power, and the Origins of Our Times*. New York, NY: Verso.

Arvidsson, A. (2006). *Brands: Meaning and Value in Media Culture*. New York, NY: Routledge.

Arvidsson, A. (2016). Facebook and finance: on the social logic of the derivative. *Theory, Culture & Society* 33 (6): 3–23.

Arvidsson, A. and Caliandro, A. (2015). Brand public. *Journal of Consumer Research* 42 (5): 727–748.

Arvidsson, A. and Colleoni, E. (2012). Value in informational capitalism and on the internet. *The Information Society* 28 (3): 135–150.

Bakshy, E., Messing, S., and Adamic, L. (2015). Exposure to ideologically diverse news and opinion on Facebook. *Science* 348 (6239): 1130–1132.

Barabasi, A. (2002). *Linked: The New Science of Networks*. Cambridge: Perseus.

Barbrook, R. (1998). The hi-tech gift economy. *First Monday* 3 (12), online.

Barbrook, R. and Cameron, A. (1996). The Californian ideology. *Science as Culture* 6 (1): 44–72.

Bardoel, J. and Deuze, M. (2001). Network journalism: converging competences of media professionals and professionalism. *Australian Journalism Review* 23 (2): 91–103.

Barlow, J.P. (1996). *A Declaration of the Independence of Cyberspace*. Electronic Frontier Foundation, online.

Bauwens, M. (2005). The political economy of peer production. *CTheory* 12 (1), online.

Baym, N. (2007). The new shape of online community: the example of Swedish independent music fandom. *First Monday* 12 (8), online.

Bell, D. (1973). *The Coming of the Post-Industrial Society*. New York, NY: Basic.

Belleflamme, P., Omrani, N., and Peitz, M. (2015). The economics of crowdfunding platforms. *Information Economics and Policy* 33: 11–28.

Benkler, Y. (2006). *The Wealth of Networks*. New Haven, CT: Yale University Press.

Bennett, L. and Segerberg, A. (2012). The logic of connective action: digital media and the personalization of contentious politics. *Information, Communication & Society* 15 (5): 739–768.

Bijker, W.E. (1997). *Of Bicycles, Bakelites, and Bulbs: Toward a Theory of Sociotechnical Change*. Cambridge, MA: MIT Press.

Birkinbine, B. (2017). From the commons to capital: Red Hat, Inc. and the business of free software. *Journal of Peer Production* 10, online.

Bishop, B. and Cushing, R. (2008). *The Big Sort: Why the Clustering of Like Minded America Is Tearing Us Apart*. Boston: Houghton Mifflin.

Bode, L., Hanna, A., Yang, J., and Shah, D.V. (2015). Candidate networks, citizen clusters, and political expression: strategic hashtag use in the 2010 midterms. *The ANNALS of the American Academy of Political and Social Science* 659 (1): 149–165.

Boepple, L. and Thompson, K. (2016). A content analytic comparison of fitspiration and thinspiration websites. *International Journal of Eating Disorders* 49 (1): 98–101.

Bogost, I. (2012). *How to Do Things with Videogames*. Minneapolis, MN: Minnesota University Press.

Boltanski, L. and Chiappello, E. (2007). *The New Spirit of Capitalism*. New York, NY: Verso.

Bolter, J.D. and Grusin, R. (2000). *Remediation: Understanding New Media*. Cambridge, MA: MIT Press.

Boyd, D. (2008). Why youth (heart) social network sites: the role of networked publics in teenage social life. In: *Youth, Identity, and Digital Media* (ed. D. Buckingham), 119–142. Cambridge, MA: MIT Press.

Boyd, D. (2010). Social network sites as networked publics: affordances, dynamics, and implications. In: *A Networked Self* (ed. Z. Papacharissi), 47–66. New York, NY: Routledge.

Boyd, D. and Ellison, N. (2007). Social network sites: definition, history, and scholarship. *Journal of Computer-Mediated Communication* 13 (1): 210–230.

Brabham, D. (2013). *Crowdsourcing*. Cambridge, MA: MIT Press.

Brophy, E. and de Peuter, G. (2014). Labours of mobility: communicative capitalism and the smartphone Cybertariat. In: *Theories of the Mobile Internet: Materialities and Imaginaries* (ed. A. Herman, J. Hadlaw and T. Swiss), 60–84. New York, NY: Routledge.

Brubaker, J., Hayes, G., and Dourish, P. (2013). Beyond the grave: Facebook as a site for the expansion of death and mourning. *The Information Society* 29 (3): 152–163.

Brunton, F. and Coleman, G. (2014). Closer to the metal. In: *Media Technologies: Essays on Communication, Materiality, and Society* (ed. T. Gillespie, P. Boczkowski and K. Foot), 77–97. Cambridge, MA: MIT Press.

Brunton, F. and Nissenbaum, H. (2015). *Obfuscation: A User's Guide for Privacy and Protest*. Cambridge, MA: MIT Press.

Burrell, J. (2016). How the machine "thinks": understanding opacity in machine learning algorithms. *Big Data & Society* 3 (1), online.

Cadwalladr, C. (2018). I made Steve Bannon's psychological warfare tool: meet the data war whistleblower. *The Guardian*, 18 March.

Caliandro, A. and Gandini, A. (2016). *Qualitative Research in Digital Environments: A Research Toolkit*. New York, NY: Routledge.

Cant, C. (2017). Precarious couriers are leading the struggle against platform capitalism. *Political Critique*, August 3.

Carpentier, N. (2012). The concept of participation: If they have access and interact, do they really participate? *Revista Fronteiras* 14 (2): 164–177.

Carpentier, N. (2016). Beyond the ladder of participation: an analytical toolkit for the critical analysis of participatory media processes. *Javnost-The Public* 23 (1): 70–88.

Casemajor, N. (2015). Digital materialisms: frameworks for digital media studies. *Westminster Papers in Communication and Culture* 10 (1): 4–17.

Casemajor, N., Couture, S., Delfin, M. et al. (2015). Non-participation in digital media: toward a framework of mediated political action. *Media, Culture & Society* 37 (6): 850–866.

Castells, M. (1996). *The Rise of the Network Society*. Oxford: Blackwell.

Castells, M. (2009). *Communication Power*. Oxford: Oxford University Press.

Ceruzzi, P. (2012). *Computing: A Concise History*. Cambridge, MA: MIT Press.

Chassany, A.S. (2016). Uber: a route out of the French banlieues. *Financial Times*, 3 March, online.

Chen, J. (2017). Thrown under the bus and outrunning it! The logic of Didi and taxi drivers' labour and activism in the on-demand economy. *New Media & Society*, online.

Cheney-Lippold, J. (2017). *We Are Data: Algorithms and the Making of Our Digital Selves*. New York, NY: NYU Press.

Cohen, N. (2008). The valorization of surveillance: towards a political economy of Facebook. *Democratic Communiqué* 22 (1): 5–22.

Cohen, N. (2016). *Writers' Rights: Freelance Journalism in a Digital Age*. Kingston, ON: McGill-Queen's University Press.

Cohen, S. (1972). *Folk Devils and Moral Panics: The Creation of Mods and Rockers*. London: McKibbon & Kee.

Coleman, G. (2005). Three ethical moments in Debian. *Social Science Research Network*, online.

Coleman, G. (2014). *Hacker, Hoaxer, Whistleblower, Spy: The Many Faces of Anonymous*. New York, NY: Verso.

Coleman, G. and Golub, A. (2008). Hacker practice: moral genres and the cultural articulation of liberalism. *Anthropological Theory* 8 (3): 255–277.

Colleoni, E., Rozza, A., and Arvidsson, A. (2014). Echo chamber or public sphere? Predicting political orientation and measuring political homophily in Twitter using big data. *Journal of Communication* 64 (2): 317–332.

Couldry, N. and Hepp, A. (2017). *The Mediated Construction of Reality*. Cambridge: Polity.

Cubitt, S. (2016). *Finite Media: Environmental Implications of Digital Technologies*. Durham, NC: Duke University Press.

Dányi, E. (2006). Xerox project: photocopy machines as a metaphor for an "open society". *The Information Society* 22 (2): 111–115.

Dean, J. (2005). Communicative capitalism: circulation and the foreclosure of politics. *Cultural Politics* 1 (1): 51–74.

Deleuze, G. (1992). Postscript on the societies of control. *October* 59: 3–7.

Delfanti, A. (2013). *Biohackers: The Politics of Open Science*. London: Pluto.

Delfanti, A. and Söderberg, J. (2018). Repurposing the hacker: three cycles of recuperation in the evolution of hacking and capitalism. *Ephemera: Theory and Politics in Organization* 18 (3), online.

Deseriis, M. (2015). *Improper Names: Collective Pseudonyms from the Luddites to Anonymous*. Minneapolis, MN: University of Minnesota Press.

Deuze, M. (2012). *Media Life*. Cambridge: Polity.

Drucker, P. (1957). *Landmarks of Tomorrow: A Report on the New "Post-Modern World".*. New York, NY: Harper.

Duchenaut, N., Yee, N., Nickell, E. et al. (2006). Alone together? Exploring the social dynamics of massively multiplayer online games. In: *Proceedings of the Sigchi Conference on Human Factors in Computing Systems*, 407–416. New York, NY: ACM Digital Library.

Duffy, B.E. (2017). *(Not) Getting Paid to Do What You Love: Gender, Social Media, and Aspirational Work.* New Haven, CT: Yale University Press.

Duffy, B.E. and Pooley, J.D. (2017). Facebook for academics: the convergence of self-branding and social media logic on Academia.edu. *Social Media + Society* 3 (1), online.

Dyer-Witheford, N. (2015). *Cyber-Proletariat: Global Labour in the Digital Vortex.* London: Pluto.

Eco, U. (1994). *Apocalypse Postponed.* Bloomington: Indiana University Press.

Edelman, B., Luca, M., and Svirsky, D. (2017). Racial discrimination in the sharing economy: evidence from a field experiment. *American Economic Journal: Applied Economics* 9 (2): 1–22.

Egenfeldt-Nielsen, S., Smith, J.H., and Tosca, S.P. (2015). *Understanding Video Games: The Essential Introduction.* New York, NY: Routledge.

Elgot, J. (2017). Momentum to launch app to get its voters out at Labour conference. *The Guardian*, 21 September.

Ert, E., Fleischer, A., and Magen, N. (2016). Trust and reputation in the sharing economy: the role of personal photos in Airbnb. *Tourism Management* 55: 62–73.

Farman, J. (2012). *Mobile Interface Theory: Embodied Space and Locative Media.* New York, NY: Routledge.

Ferguson, J. (1990). *The Anti-Politics Machine: "Development," Depoliticization and Bureaucratic Power in Lesotho.* Cambridge: Cambridge University Press.

Florida, R. (2002). *The Rise of the Creative Class, and How It's Transforming Work, Leisure and Everyday Life.* New York, NY: Basic.

Ford, H. and Wajcman, J. (2017). "Anyone can edit," not everyone does: Wikipedia's infrastructure and the gender gap. *Social Studies of Science* 47 (4): 511–527.

Foucault, M. (1977). *Discipline and Punish: The Birth of the Prison.* New York: Vintage.

Friedman, B. and Nissembaum, H. (1997). Bias in computer systems. In: *Human Values and the Design of Computer Technology* (ed. B. Friedman), 21–40. Cambridge: Cambridge University Press.

Gandini, A. (2015). The rise of coworking spaces: a literature review. *Ephemera* 15 (1): 193–205.

Gandini, A. (2016). *The Reputation Economy: Understanding Knowledge Work in Digital Society.* London: Palgrave Macmillan.

Gardiner, B., Mansfield, M., Anderson, I. et al. (2016). The dark side of *Guardian* comments. *The Guardian*, online.

Gates, B. (1976). Open letter to the hobbyists. *Homebrew Computer Club Newsletter* 2 (1): 2.

Gerbaudo, P. (2012). *Tweets and the Streets: Social Media and Contemporary Activism.* London: Pluto Press.

Gerbaudo, P. (2016). Social media teams as digital vanguards: the question of leadership in the management of key Facebook and Twitter accounts of Occupy Wall Street, Indignados and UK Uncut. *Information, Communication & Society* 1–18, online.

Gerbaudo, P. (2018). *The Digital Party: Political Organisation in the Era of Social Media*. London: Pluto Press.

Gerbaudo, P. and Treré, E. (2015). In search of the "we" of social media activism: introduction to the special issue on social media and protest identities. *Information, Communication and Society* 18 (8): 865–871.

Gill, R. (2007). *Gender and the Media*. Cambridge: Polity.

Gillespie, T. (2010). The politics of "platforms". *New Media & Society* 12 (3): 347–364.

Gillespie, T. (2014). The relevance of algorithms. In: *Media Technologies: Essays on Communication, Materiality, and Society* (ed. T. Gillespie, P. Boczkowski and K. Foot), 167–194. Cambridge, MA: MIT Press.

Gilpin, R. (2001). *Global Political Economy: Understanding the International Economic Order*. Princeton, NJ: Princeton University Press.

Gitelman, L. and Pingree, G. (2003). What's new about new media. In: *New Media 1740–1915* (ed. L. Gitelman and G. Pingree), xi–xxii. Cambridge, MA: MIT Press.

Gleick, J. (2011). *The Information: A History, a Theory, a Flood*. New York, NY: Pantheon.

Goerzen, M. (2017). Notes toward the memes of production. *Texte Zur Kunst* 106: 82–108.

Goffman, E. (1959). *The Presentation of Self in Everyday Life*. Garden City: Doubleday.

Goldstein, E. (2008). *The Best of 2600: A Hacker Odyssey*. Hoboken, NJ: Wiley.

Goode, L. (2009). Social news, citizen journalism and democracy. *New Media & Society* 11 (8): 1287–1305.

Graham, M. and Anwar, M.A. (2018). Digital labor. In: *Digital Geographies* (ed. J. Ash, R. Kitchin and A. Leszczynski). London: Sage, in press.

Grainge, P. (ed.) (2012). *Ephemeral Media: Transitory Screen Culture from Television to YouTube*. New York, NY: Springer.

Greenpeace (2017). *Clicking Clean: Who Is Winning the Race to Build a Green Internet?* Washington, DC: Greenpeace Inc.

Greenwald, G. (2014). *No Place to Hide: Edward Snowden, the NSA, and the US Surveillance State*. London: Macmillan.

Gregg, M. (2011). *Work's Intimacy*. Cambridge: Polity.

Grossman, G.M. and Helpman, E. (1994). Endogenous innovation in the theory of growth. *Journal of Economic Perspectives* 8 (1): 23–44.

Habermas, J. (1984). *The Theory of Communicative Action*. Boston, MA: Beacon.

Haight, M., Quan-Haase, A., and Corbett, B.A. (2014). Revisiting the digital divide in Canada: the impact of demographic factors on access to the internet, level of online activity, and social networking site usage. *Information, Communication & Society* 17 (4): 503–519.

Hamari, J., Sjöklint, M., and Ukkonen, A. (2016). The sharing economy: why people participate in collaborative consumption. *Journal of the Association for Information Science and Technology* 67 (9): 2047–2059.

Harding, L. (2016). What are the Panama Papers? A guide to history's biggest data leak. *The Guardian*, 5 April.

Hardt, M. and Negri, A. (2000). *Empire*. Cambridge, MA: Harvard University Press.

Hargittai, E. and Hinnant, A. (2008). Digital inequality differences in young adults' use of the internet. *Communication Research* 35 (5): 602–621.

Harrison, T.M. and Barthel, B. (2009). Wielding new media in Web 2.0: exploring the history of engagement with the collaborative construction of media products. *New Media & Society* 11 (1–2): 155–178.

Harvey, D. (2005). *A Brief History of Neoliberalism*. Oxford: Oxford University Press.

Hasinoff, A. (2012). Sexting as media production: rethinking social media and sexuality. *New Media & Society* 15 (4): 449–465.

Haythornthwaite, C. (2002). Strong, weak, and latent ties and the impact of new media. *The Information Society* 18 (5): 385–401.

Hearn, A. (2008). Meat, mask, burden: probing the contours of the branded self. *Journal of Consumer Culture* 8 (2): 197–217.

Hess, C. and Ostrom, E. (ed.) (2007). *Understanding Knowledge as a Commons*. Cambridge, MA: MIT Press.

Hesse, C. (2002). The rise of intellectual property, 700 BC–AD 2000: an idea in the balance. *Daedalus* 131 (2): 26–45.

Himanen, P. (2001). *The Hacker Ethic: A Radical Approach to the Philosophy of Business*. New York, NY: Random House.

Hindman, E.B. and Thomas, R.J. (2014). When old and new media collide: the case of WikiLeaks. *New Media & Society* 16 (4): 541–558.

Hosanagar, K., Fleder, D., Lee, D. et al. (2014). Will the global village fracture into tribes? Recommender systems and their effects on consumer fragmentation. *Management Science* 60 (4): 805–823.

Howard, P., Savage, S., Saviaga, C. et al. (2016). Social media, civic engagement, and the Slacktivism hypothesis: lessons from Mexico's El Bronco. *Journal of International Affairs* 70 (1): 55–73.

Huston, L. and Sakkab, N. (2006). Connect and develop: inside Procter & Gamble's new model for innovation. *Harvard Business Review* 84 (3): 58–66.

Huws, U. (2014). *Labor in the Global Digital Economy*. New York, NY: Monthly Review Press.

Hyde, A., Linksvayer, M., Kanarinka et al. (2012). What is collaboration anyway? In: *The Social Media Reader* (ed. M. Mandiberg), 53–67. New York, NY: New York University Press.

Illouz, E. (2007). *Cold Intimacies: The Making of Emotional Capitalism*. Cambridge: Polity.

Innis, H. (1950). *Empire and Communications*. Oxford: Clarendon.

Ippolita (2005). *Open non è free*. Milan: Eleuthera.

Irani, L. (2015). The cultural work of microwork. *New Media & Society* 17 (5): 720–739.

Jacobson, J., Lin, C.Z., and McEwen, R. (2017). Aging with technology: seniors and mobile connections. *Canadian Journal of Communication* 42 (2), online.

Jarrett, K. (2003). Labour of love: an archaeology of affect as power in E-commerce. *Journal of Sociology* 39 (4): 335–351.

Jasanoff, S. (ed.) (2004). *States of Knowledge: The Co-Production of Science and the Social Order*. New York, NY: Routledge.

Jenkins, H. (2006). *Convergence Culture*. New York, NY: New York University Press.

Johns, A. (2009). *Piracy: The Intellectual Property Wars from Gutenberg to Gates*. Chicago: University of Chicago Press.

Karppi, T. (2018). *Disconnect: Facebook's Affective Bonds*. Minneapolis, MN: University of Minnesota Press.

Kelty, C. (2008). *Two Bits: The Cultural Significance of Free Software*. Durham, NC: Duke University Press.

Kelty, C. (2016). Participation. In: *Digital Keywords* (ed. B. Peters), 227–241. Princeton, NJ: Princeton University Press.

Kenney, M. and Zysman, J. (2016). The rise of the platform economy. *Issues in Science and Technology* 32 (3): 61–69.

Kim, J. (2012). The institutionalization of YouTube: from user-generated content to professionally generated content. *Media, Culture & Society* 34 (1): 53–67.

Kraemer, K.L., Dedrick, J., and Sharma, P. (2009). One laptop per child: vision vs. reality. *Communications of the ACM* 52 (6): 66–73.

Kramer, A., Guillory, J., and Hancock, J. (2014). Experimental evidence of massive-scale emotional contagion through social networks. *Proceedings of the National Academy of Sciences* 111 (24): 8788–8790.

Kuehn, K. and Corrigan, T.F. (2013). Hope labor: the role of employment prospects in online social production. *The Political Economy of Communication* 1 (1): 9–25.

Kumar, K. (1995). *From Post-Industrial to Post-Modern Society: New Theories of the Contemporary World*. New York, NY: Blackwell.

Lakhani, K. and Wolf, R. (2003). Why hackers do what they do: understanding motivation and effort in free/open source software projects. MIT Sloan Working Paper No. 4425–03.

Lanier, J. (2010). *You Are Not a Gadget: A Manifesto*. New York, NY: Knopf.

Lanier, J. (2014). *Who Owns the Future?* New York, NY: Simon and Schuster.

Lauterbach, D., Truong, H., Shah, T. et al. (2009). Surfing a web of trust: reputation and reciprocity on couchsurfing.com. *Computational Science and Engineering* 4: 346–353.

Lee, M.K., Kusbit, D., Metsky, E. et al. (2015). Working with machines: the impact of algorithmic and data-driven management on human workers. In: *Proceedings of the 33rd Annual ACM Conference on Human Factors in Computing Systems*, 1603–1612.

Lepore, J. (2014). The disruption machine. *The New Yorker* 23: 30–36.

Lessig, L. (2002). *The Future of Ideas: The Fate of the Commons in a Connected World*. New York, NY: Random House.

Levine, R., Locke, C., Searls, D. et al. (2000). *The Cluetrain Manifesto: The End of Business as Usual*. Cambridge: Perseus Books.

Lévy, P. (1997). *Collective Intelligence: Mankind's Emerging World in Cyberspace*. Cambridge: Perseus Books.

Levy, S. (2001). *Hackers: Heroes of the Computer Revolution*. New York: Penguin.

Levy, S. (2011). *In the Plex: How Google Thinks, Works, and Shapes Our Lives*. New York, NY: Simon & Schuster.

Light, J. (1999). When computers were women. *Technology and Culture* 40 (3): 455–483.

Lindtner, S., Greenspan, A., and Li, D. (2015). Designed in Shenzhen: Shanzhai manufacturing and maker entrepreneurs. *Proceedings of The Fifth Decennial Aarhus Conference on Critical Alternatives*: 85–96.

Lotan, G., Graeff, E., Ananny, M. et al. (2011). The revolutions were tweeted: information flows during the 2011 Tunisian and Egyptian revolutions. *International Journal of Communication* 5: 1375–1405.

Lury, C. (2011). *Consumer Culture*. New Brunswick, NJ: Rutgers University Press.

Lyon, D. (2014). Surveillance, Snowden, and big data: capacities, consequences, critique. *Big Data & Society* 1 (2): 1–13.

Magaudda, P. (2010). Hacking practices and their relevance for consumer studies: the example of the "Jailbreaking" of the iPhone. *Consumers, Commodities and Consumption* 12 (1).

Manovich, L. (2001). *The Language of New Media*. Cambridge, MA: MIT Press.

Marwick, A.E. and Boyd, D. (2014). Networked privacy: how teenagers negotiate context in social media. *New Media & Society* 16 (7): 1051–1067.

Marx, K. (1993). *Grundrisse: Foundations of the Critique of Political Economy*. New York, NY: Penguin.

Matamoros-Fernandez, A. (2017). Platformed racism: the mediation and circulation of an Australian race-based controversy on Twitter, Facebook and YouTube. *Information, Communication & Society* 20 (6): 930–946.

Mattelart, A. (2003). *The Information Society: An Introduction*. London: Sage.

McEwen, K.D. (2017). Self-tracking practices and digital (re)productive labour. *Philosophy & Technology* 31 (2): 235–251.

McLuhan, M. (1962). *The Gutenberg Galaxy: The Making of Typographic Man*. Toronto: University of Toronto Press.

McLuhan, M. (1964). *Understanding Media: The Extensions of Man*. New York, NY: McGraw-Hill.

McQuail, D. (1969). *Towards a Sociology of Mass Communications*. London: Macmillan.

Medina, E. (2011). *Cybernetic Revolutionaries: Technology and Politics in Allende's Chile*. Cambridge, MA: MIT Press.

Milner, R. (2013). Hacking the social: internet memes, identity antagonism, and the logic of lulz. *The Fibreculture Journal* 22: 62–92, online.

Moore, G. (1965). Cramming more components onto integrated circuits. *Electronics* 38 (8).

Morini, C. (2007). The feminization of labour in cognitive capitalism. *Feminist Review* 87: 40–59.

Morozov, E. (2011). *The Net Delusion: The Dark Side of Internet Freedom*. New York, NY: PublicAffairs.

Mosco, V. (2004). *The Digital Sublime. Myth, Power, and Cyberspace*. Cambridge, MA: MIT Press.

Moulier Boutang, Y. (ed.) (2011). *Cognitive Capitalism*. Cambridge: Polity.

Mueller, M.L. (2010). *Networks and States: The Global Politics of Internet Governance*. Cambridge, MA: MIT Press.

Muniz, A.M. and O'Guinn, T.C. (2001). Brand community. *Journal of Consumer Research* 27 (4): 412–432.

Musiani, F. (2012). Caring about the plumbing: on the importance of architectures in social studies of (peer-to-peer) technology. *Journal of Peer Production* 1: 1–8.

Nakamura, L. (2002). *Cybertypes: Race, Ethnicity, and Identity on the Internet*. New York, NY: Routledge.

Nakamura, L. (2008). *Digitizing Race: Visual Cultures of the Internet*. Minneapolis, MN: University of Minnesota Press.

Navas, E. (2012). *Remix Theory: The Aesthetics of Sampling*. New York, NY: Springer.

Negroponte, N. (1995). *Being Digital*. New York, NY: Knopf.

Nielsen, M.A. (2012). *Reinventing Discovery: The New Era of Networked Science*. Princeton, NJ: Princeton University Press.

Noam, E.M. (2016). *Who Owns the World's Media?: Media Concentration and Ownership Around the World*. Oxford: Oxford University Press.

Noble, D. (2017). *Forces of Production: A Social History of Industrial Automation*. New York, NY: Routledge.

Noble, S.U. (2018). *Algorithms of Oppression: How Search Engines Reinforce Racism*. New York, NY: NYU Press.

Norman, D.A. (1999). Affordance, conventions, and design. *Interactions* 6 (3): 38–43.

Norris, P. (2001). *Digital Divide: Civic Engagement, Information Poverty, and the Internet Worldwide*. Cambridge: Cambridge University Press.

Okolloh, O. (2009). Ushahidi, or "testimony": Web 2.0 tools for crowdsourcing crisis information. *Participatory Learning and Action* 59 (1): 65–70.

O'Neil, M. (2009). *Cyberchiefs: Autonomy and Authority in Online Tribes*. London: Pluto.

O'Reilly, T. (2005). What is Web 2.0? O'Reilly.com, online.

Oudshoorn, N.E. and Pinch, T. (ed.) (2003). *How Users Matter: The Co-Construction of Users and Technologies*. Cambridge, MA: MIT Press.

Pantzar, M. (1997). Domestication of everyday life technology: dynamic views on the social histories of artifacts. *Design Issues* 13 (3): 52–65.

Papacharissi, Z. (2002). The virtual sphere: the internet as a public sphere. *New Media & Society* 4 (1): 9–27.

Papacharissi, Z. (ed.) (2010). *A Networked Self: Identity, Community, and Culture on Social Network Sites*. New York, NY: Routledge.

Papacharissi, Z. (2016). Affective publics and structures of storytelling: sentiment, events and mediality. *Information, Communication & Society* 19 (3): 307–324.

Parikka, J. (2013). *What Is Media Archaeology*. Hoboken, NJ: Wiley.

Pateman, C. (1970). *Participation and Democratic Theory*. Cambridge: Cambridge University Press.

Paulussen, S. and Harder, R.A. (2014). Social media references in newspapers: Facebook, Twitter and YouTube as sources in newspaper journalism. *Journalism Practice* 8 (5): 542–551.

Peck, J. (2005). Struggling with the creative class. *International Journal of Urban and Regional Research* 29 (4): 740–770.

Peters, B. (2016). *How to Not Network a Nation*. Cambridge, MA: MIT Press.

Plaut, E. (2015). Technologies of avoidance: the swear jar and the cell phone. *First Monday* 20 (11), online.

Portwood-Stacer, L. (2012). Media refusal and conspicuous non-consumption: the performative and political dimensions of Facebook abstention. *New Media & Society* 15 (7): 1041–1057.

Prensky, M. (2001). Digital natives, digital immigrants. *On the Horizon* 9 (5): 1–6.

Putnam, R.D. (2000). *Bowling Alone: The Collapse and Revival of American Community*. New York, NY: Simon & Schuster.

Rainie, H. and Wellman, B. (2012). *Networked: The New Social Operating System*. Cambridge, MA: MIT Press.

Raymond, E. (1999). Linux and open-source success. *IEEE Software* 16 (1): 85–89.

Reagle, J. and Rhue, L. (2011). Gender bias in Wikipedia and Britannica. *International Journal of Communication* 5: 1138–1158.

Renninger, B.J. (2015). "Where I can be myself … where I can speak my mind": networked counterpublics in a polymedia environment. *New Media & Society* 17 (9): 1513–1529.

Rheingold, H. (2003). *Smart Mobs: The Next Social Revolution*. Cambridge: Perseus Books.

Rifkin, J. (2011). *The Third Industrial Revolution*. London: Palgrave Macmillan.

Rivera, J.L. and Lallmahomed, A. (2016). Environmental implications of planned obsolescence and product lifetime: a literature review. *International Journal of Sustainable Engineering* 9 (2): 119–129.

Roberts, S. (2016). Commercial content moderation: digital laborers' dirty work. In: *The Intersectional Internet: Race, Sex, Class, and Culture Online* (ed. S. Noble and B. Tynes), 147–160. New York, NY: Peter Lang.

Rogers, R. (2013). *Digital Methods*. Cambridge, MA: MIT Press.

Rosenblat, A. and Stark, L. (2016). Algorithmic labor and information asymmetries: a case study of Uber's drivers. *International Journal of Communication* 10: 3758–3784.

Rosenzweig, R. (1998). Wizards, bureaucrats, warriors, and hackers: writing the history of the internet. *The American Historical Review* 103 (5): 1530–1552.

Ross, A. (2012). In search of the lost paycheck. In: *Digital Labor: The Internet as Playground and Factory* (ed. T. Scholz), 21–40. New York, NY: Routledge.

Ross, A. (2017). Working for nothing: the latest high-growth sector? In: *Mapping Precariousness, Labour Insecurity and Uncertain Livelihoods* (ed. E. Armano, A. Bove and A. Murgia), 189–198. New York, NY: Routledge.

Roth, L. (2009). Looking at Shirley, the ultimate norm: colour balance, image technologies, and cognitive equity. *Canadian Journal of Communication* 34 (1): 111–136.

Rushkoff, D. (2016). *Throwing Rocks at the Google Bus: How Growth Became the Enemy of Prosperity*. New York, NY: Penguin.

Ryan, J. (2010). *A History of the Internet and the Digital Future*. London: Reaktion.

Schiller, D. (2000). *Digital Capitalism: Networking the Global Market System*. Cambridge, MA: MIT Press.

Scholz, T. (2016a). *Platform Cooperativism: Challenging the Corporate Sharing Economy*. New York, NY: Rosa Luxembourg Stiftung.

Scholz, T. (2016b). *Uberworked and Underpaid: How Workers Are Disrupting the Digital Economy*. Hoboken, NJ: Wiley.

Schor, J., Walker, E., Lee, C. et al. (2015). On the sharing economy. *Contexts* 14 (1): 12–19.

Seaver, N. (2017). Algorithms as culture: some tactics for the ethnography of algorithmic systems. *Big Data & Society* 4 (2), online.

Selby, A. (2017). Timed toilet breaks, impossible targets and workers falling asleep on feet: brutal life working in Amazon warehouse. *Mirror*, 25 November.

Sennett, R. (1998). *The Corrosion of Character: The Personal Consequences of Work in the New Capitalism*. New York, NY: Norton.

Sevignani, S. (2016). The problem of privacy in capitalism and alternative social media: the case of diaspora. In: *Marx in the Age of Digital Capitalism* (ed. C. Fuchs and V. Mosco), 413–446. Leiden: Brill.

Sharma, S. (2018). *TaskRabbit: The Gig Economy and Finding Time to Care Less*. Preprint.

Shirky, C. (2010). *Cognitive Surplus: Creativity and Generosity in a Connected Age*. New York, NY: Penguin.

Simmel, G. (1908). *Soziologie*. Leipzig: Duncker & Humblot.

Sismondo, S. (2011). *An Introduction to Science and Technology Studies*. New York, NY: Wiley Blackwell.

Smiley, L. (2015). The shut-in economy. *Medium*, online.

Smith, C. (2010). Google Ceo Eric Schmidt's most controversial quotes about privacy. *The Huffington Post*, 11 April.

Smith, C., Attwood, F., and Barker, M. (2015). Queering porn audiences. In: *Queer Sex Work* (ed. M. Laing, K. Pilcher and N. Smith), 177–188. New York, NY: Routledge.

Söderberg, J. and Daoud, A. (2012). Atoms want to be free too! Expanding the critique of intellectual property to physical goods. *tripleC: Communication, Capitalism & Critique* 10 (1): 66–76.

Srnicek, N. (2016). *Platform Capitalism*. Cambridge: Polity.

Stalder, F. (2006). *Manuel Castells: The Theory of the Network Society*. Cambridge: Polity.

Stalder, F. (2018). *The Digital Condition*. Cambridge: Polity.

Stallman, R. (1986). *The Free Software Definition*. Free Software Foundation.

Standing, G. (2011). *The Precariat: The New Dangerous Class*. London: Bloomsbury Academic.

Stearns, P.N. (2016). *Globalization in World History*. New York, NY: Routledge.

Steiner, C. and Dixon, W. (2012). *Automate This: How Algorithms Came to Rule Our World*. New York: Penguin.

Sunstein, C. (2001). *Republic.com*. Princeton, NJ: Princeton University Press.

Swan, M. (2015). *Blockchain: Blueprint for a New Economy*. Sebastopol: O'Reilly Media.

Terranova, T. (2000). Free labor: producing culture for the digital economy. *Social Text* 18 (2): 33–58.

Tkacz, N. (2015). *Wikipedia and the Politics of Openness*. Chicago: University of Chicago Press.

Toffler, A. (1980). *The Third Wave: The Classic Study of Tomorrow*. New York, NY: Bantam.

Tomaney, J. (1994). A new paradigm of work organization and technology? In: *Post-Fordism: A Reader* (ed. A. Amin), 157–194. New York: Wiley.

Tönnies, F. (1912). *Gemeinschaft und gesellschaft: Grundbegriffe der reinen soziologie*. Berlino: Cutius.

Touraine, A. (1971). *The Post-Industrial Society*. New York, NY: Random House.

Truitt, B. (2014). "Empire Strikes Back Uncut" mash-up video debuts Friday. *USA Today*, 9 October.

Turkle, S. (2008). Always-on/always-on-you: the tethered self. In: *Handbook of Mobile Communication Studies* (ed. J. Katz), 121–137. Cambridge, MA: MIT Press.

Turkle, S. (2011). *Alone Together: Why We Expect More from Technology and Less from Each Other*. New York, NY: Basic.

Turner, F. (2006). *From Counterculture to Cyberculture: Stewart Brand, the Whole Earth Network and the Rise of Digital Utopianism*. Chicago: University of Chicago Press.

Turner, F. (2009). Burning Man at Google: a cultural infrastructure for new media production. *New Media & Society* 11 (1–2): 73–94.

Tushnet, R. (2017). Copyright law, fan practices, and the rights of the author. In: *Fandom: Identities and Communities in a Mediated World* (ed. J. Gray, C. Sandvoss and C.L. Harrington), 77–90. New York, NY: NYU Press.

Van der Graaf, S. (2018). *ComMODify: User Creativity at the Intersection of Commerce and Community*. London: Palgrave Macmillan.

Van Dijck, J. (2013a). "You have one identity": performing the self on Facebook and LinkedIn. *Media, Culture & Society* 35 (2): 199–215.

Van Dijck, J. (2013b). *The Culture of Connectivity: A Critical History of Social Media*. Oxford: Oxford University Press.

Van Dijck, J. and Hacker, K. (2011). The digital divide as a complex and dynamic phenomenon. *The Information Society* 19 (4): 315–326.

Van Doorn, N. (2017). Platform labor: on the gendered and racialized exploitation of low-income service work in the "on-demand" economy. *Information, Communication & Society* 20 (6): 898–914.

Vanolo, A. (2014). Smartmentality: the smart city as disciplinary strategy. *Urban Studies* 51 (5): 883–898.

Veugen, C. (2016). Assassin's creed and Transmedia storytelling. *International Journal of Gaming and Computer-Mediated Simulations* 8 (2): 1–19.

Vonderau, P. (2017). The Spotify effect: digital distribution and financial growth. *Television & New Media*, online.

Wagner, J. (2016). Clinton's data-driven campaign relied heavily on an algorithm named Ada: what didn't she see? *The Washington Post*, 9 November.

Wajcman, J. (2000). Reflections on gender and technology studies: in what state is the art? *Social Studies of Science* 30 (3): 447–464.

Wallace, J. (2017). Modelling contemporary gatekeeping. *Digital Journalism* 6 (3): 274–293.

Warner, M. (2002). Publics and counterpublics. *Public Culture* 14 (1): 49–90.

Weaver, D.H. and Willnat, L. (2016). Changes in US journalism: how do journalists think about social media? *Journalism Practice* 10 (7): 844–855.

Webster, F. (2014). *Theories of the Information Society*. New York, NY: Routledge.

Winner, L. (1980). Do artifacts have politics? *Daedalus* 109 (1): 121–136.

Woolgar, S. (1990). Configuring the user: the case of usability trials. *The Sociological Review* 38 (1_suppl): 58–99.

Wu, T. (2010). *The Master Switch: The Rise and Fall of Information Empires*. New York, NY: Knopf.

Wyatt, S.M., Oudshoorn, N., and Pinch, T. (2003). Non-users also matter: the construction of users and non-users of the internet. In: *How Users Matter: The Co-Construction of Users and Technology* (ed. N. Oudshoorn and T. Pinch), 67–79. Cambridge, MA: MIT Press.

Xu, B. and Li, D. (2015). An empirical study of the motivations for content contribution and community participation in Wikipedia. *Information & Management* 52 (3): 275–286.

Zittrain, J., Faris, R., Noman, H. et al. (2017). The Shifting Landscape of Global Internet Censorship. Berkman Klein Center Research Publication No. 2017–4.

Zuboff, S. (2016). The secrets of surveillance capitalism. *Frankfurter Allgemeine*, 5 March.

Index

The *italic* page numbers refer to boxes and **bold** to glossary terms.

Introduction to Digital Media, First Edition. Alessandro Delfanti and Adam Arvidsson.
© 2019 John Wiley & Sons, Inc. Published 2019 by John Wiley & Sons, Inc.